TEXAS SAFARI
The Game Hunter's Guide to Texas

TEXAS SAFARI

THE GAME HUNTER'S GUIDE TO TEXAS

GAYNE C. YOUNG

JOHN M. HARDY PUBLISHING

ALPINE & HOUSTON

2007

First Printing: October 2007

ISBN 0-9717667-9-7

Printed and Bound in the United States of America

Cover Design: Vast Graphics, Alpine, Texas

Cover Photo Credits:
Mule deer (top) - Texas Parks and Wildlife Department
Axis deer (left) - Gayne C. Young
Bowhunter (center) - Paul Harris, Brush Country Camo
Jaguar hunt (bottom center) - David J. Schmidly
Feral hog (right center) - Cody Weiser
Pronghorn (bottom right) - Jessie Martinez, Bushlan Camo

John M. Hardy Publishing
Houston, Texas

www.johnmhardy.com

For Big Joe

Contents

FOREWORD

In the world of writing, there is a thin line between presenting information in a boring or in a fascinating manner. As a research biologist, outdoor writer, author and speaker, I feel like there are times when I've strayed on either side of that fine line. As a writer, and especially a reader, I truly appreciate someone who, through talent, can remain on the fascinating side of the line. Gayne Young is such a writer.

I first ran across Gayne Young's writing in *Sporting Classics Magazine,* one of the very few outdoor publications I personally subscribe to and where I serve as the "LongHunter" columnist. The story Gayne told was about the last jaguar taken in Texas. Reading his words, I felt like I had been part of that history. And when I was finished with the tale, it left me wanting more of his stories involving both history and good storytelling. What you're about to read is what I've been looking for, and I suspect a whole lot of other folks have been looking for as well, both here within the boundaries of Texas, but also well beyond.

To say you're in for a most interesting, rewarding and timeless journey is an understatement. Read and enjoy what follows—I did. But once again Gayne Young has left me wanting more of his writing!

Larry Weishuhn
Uvalde, Texas

ACKNOWLEDGEMENTS

Before I begin to tackle this section of the book, I'd like to give special thanks to my wife, Karen. Thank you for everything. You are the love of my life, but I will surely burn in hell for what I've put you and the kids through during the writing of this book.

The acknowledgements page in nonfiction books is generally a pretty dull affair. Usually, the author rambles on about his or her muse or the undying love and support from someone who never gave up on them even after a pile of rejection letters.

So rather than follow the norm, I'll just jot down a list of the people who helped me the most with this project.

Thanks to Mike Scooby at *Gander Mountain* for his guidance and introductions. Thanks to Chuck Wechsler at *Sporting Classics*, Diana Rupp and Mike Few at *Sports Field* and Doug Hewlett at *Outdoor Life*; without y'all I'd be standing on a street corner somewhere holding a sign that reads, "Will write for food."

Thanks to Larry Weishuhn of Uvalde for writing the foreword.

Thanks to Richard Sanders at *Russell Moccasins* and *Walden Bork*, Jin Laxmidas at *TAG Safari*, Eddie Stevensen at *Remington*, Richard Gilligan at *Meopta*, Reed Berry at *TZ Case*, Jeff Wemmer at *Texas Hunt Co.* and Chris Cashbaugh at *SOG Knives*. Your generous support provided me with products that make me at least appear to know what I'm doing.

Thanks to Garry Wright of *Garry Wright Safaris* for his guidance and tender words of wisdom.

Thanks to Neal Coldwell of Neal Coldwell Taxidermy for his instruction and for showing me the true meaning of class.

Thanks to Ken Wilson of *Sportsmen on Film* for always answering my questions, no matter how annoying they may be.

Thanks to Maria Ramos and the rest of the staff at the Pioneer Memorial Library in Fredericksburg, Texas, for helping me track down every obscure book I asked for.

Thanks to Joel O'Shoney and *PakMail Taylor* for being a friend and for taking care of my shipping needs. Thanks also to his wife, Juliet, for her even-keeled patience and calm demeanor.

Thanks to the families of Will Crowe, Champe Carter and Dr. Creighton Miller. And thanks to the many, many people I've failed to list here. Not because I've forgotten about you, but because you already know what you mean to me.

Gayne C. Young
Fredericksburg, Texas

PREFACE

I suppose that I was first drawn to hunting through my early childhood days spent in front of the television. Watching movies such as *King Kong, Mogambo* and *King Solomon's Mines*, I became fascinated with the men who ventured into the unknown corners of the world with only a rifle in their hand and khaki on their back in search of adventure. Even though the action was exaggerated, and in the case of *King Kong* complete fantasy, I knew from then on that hunting and adventure were synonymous. My childhood play was centered on this belief, and I often explored the woods near my grandparent's house with air rifle in hand, expecting a death charge from imaginary animals at any moment.

Later, I took more personal and descriptive adventures with the likes of Corbett, Capstick, Roosevelt and Hemingway. With their words guiding me, I hunted man-eating tigers in India, took the Big Five many times over and spent a year traveling the Dark Continent collecting trophy after trophy for museums. Reading these works over and over again only fueled my desire to experience such adventures first hand. Unfortunately, in my teenage years, trips to Africa and India weren't financially feasible. Not one to be discouraged, I looked to my own big backyard.

The Texas I found could offer just as much as those faraway places and for a much cheaper price. With help from my father's friends, I went deer hunting in the almost impenetrable darkness of the pineywoods in the eastern portion of the state. Like I do with all my trips, I researched the location beforehand and found an area steeped in hunting history. Bears, cats, deer and hogs were all once found in the Big Thicket area and traipsing through the woods near Diboll, I couldn't help but feel that parts of the region were unchanged. Although those hunts were on private land or leased land, my real Texas safaris began when I discovered the public hunting lands managed by the Texas Parks and Wildlife Department. My first foray into the state-managed land system fulfilled all my dreams and then some.

It was at Mad Island Wildlife Management Area. Less than an hour after arriving, I found myself wading through chest-high slime looking for a suitable place to bait for alligator. The reward for all my hours of carrying rotting flesh through the leech-infested waters turned out to be a new refuge record: a 12-foot, 4-inch bull alligator that weighed more than 600 pounds.

The rewards continued, because that experience marked the beginning of my career as a writer, with sales to *Texas Fish & Game* and *American Hunter*. From then on, I entered every public drawing the state offered. And although the majority of my applications ended with my failing to be drawn, I have been lucky enough to hunt some of the greatest and wildest areas the state has to offer.

At Big Bend State Ranch on the border with Mexico, I hunted free-ranging aoudad and ibex on more than 6,000 acres of deep canyons and draws. A friend and I had the area to ourselves, and park personnel gave us a stern warning to watch out for drug smugglers crossing through the area. Who wouldn't think that hunting in such a remote place with the threat of encountering smugglers isn't an adventure?

On a javelina hunt at Black Gap Wildlife Management Area, I was greeted with literature that read, **"Watch for venomous snakes, insects, mountain lions, black bears and flash flooding."** Having avoided those dangers during a hard day afield, I retired to my tent to pull thorns from my shins and cool my sunburned skin only to have the temperature drop to below freezing in a matter of hours. While hunting the Chaparral for feral hogs, I happily gave my tent to a 6-foot rattlesnake rather than share it. And on a return trip to Mad Island for alligator, the mosquitoes were so thick I probably inhaled more than bit me.

In addition to public hunts, I have been fortunate to hunt deer, javelina, hog, predators and free ranging exotics on some of the best managed privately held land in Texas. I have also spent time on some game ranches where I saw more game in a day than I thought possible and was fed and treated like a king.

Hunting and writing have taken me halfway around the world, from Africa to New Guinea, but for me there is no land that holds as much potential for a great time as Texas. Hunting means different things to different people. For some it is a way to acquire food. For others it is a sport. Some view it as a competition, while others who go afield could care less if they take anything at all.

For me, hunting has always been about the adventure and the stories that come with it, about time in the wild with close friends and then talking about it the next time we're together.

With more than 260,000 square miles, opportunities for almost every type of hunting imaginable, and a plethora of species, Texas is a hunter's paradise. In addition to native species, Texas is also home to a large number of species transplanted from Europe, Africa and Asia. Of these "exotics," some are free ranging while others are found behind game fences on large ranches. Regardless of their location, the opportunity for fair and ethical hunting exists for all of them.

Whatever your reason for hunting, whatever game you choose to hunt and whether you're a native Texan or visiting the state for the first time, I hope this book helps guide you to a great time afield.

INTRODUCTION

Divided into 10 vegetational regions, Texas offers hunters a tremendous choice of game and topography. From the deserts in the west, to the pine thickets in the east, to the Gulf Coastal plains, Texas is a land of extremes. This abundance of land was one of the saving graces of the new government when Texas became an independent Republic in 1836. Property that was sold at extremely low prices lured new settlers and in turn helped finance the Republic of Texas. More than 150 years later, the majority of Texas land is still privately held.

Hunting in Texas is big business and more and more landowners and ranchers are supplementing their income by allowing hunters to *lease* their land for hunting privileges. This leasing program has a long history in Texas and the majority of deer taken in the state is through this arrangement. Leases can be fairly inexpensive to astronomical, depending upon the location of the lease, the type of game available and the management program in place.

Another way landowners can benefit from hunting is by "game ranching." Here ranch owners manage native species and introduce new species for safari-style hunting. Accommodations and cost vary by ranch. Some offer simple bunkhouse style lodging where guests provide their own linens and cook for themselves while others offer private bungalows with room service and meals created by classically trained chefs. Some of the larger and more professional game ranches are listed in Chapter 7.

Considering the fact that more than 90 percent of the land in Texas is privately held, hunters might think that the state has little in the way of hunting on public land. Quite the opposite is true. Texas has millions of acres of public hunting available through such entities as Texas Parks and Wildlife, the Federal Government, the Army Corps of Engineers and city and county municipalities. Some of this land is available to hunters by on-site registration and some requires a lottery type drawing. Information about hunting on public land, including species available for hunting, and registration requirements are found in Chapter 7.

In the chapters dealing with game, readers will find information and history on each species, the best places to hunt, popular methods of hunting and recommended calibers. There are also sections on some non-game species, exotic animals that have made Texas their home, endangered species and animals that, although science has never confirmed it, some Texans swear they've encountered. Other chapters offer advice and suggestions on clothing as well as things that can make a hunter's life miserable, such as poisonous insects and plants.

In short, this book is for anyone who hunts, has a fascination with hunting history, the Texas outdoors, adventure, or who is searching for the trophy of a lifetime.

And on a final note …

You can always tell a Texan, but you can't tell him much.
— Popular Saying

The information in this book was compiled from a variety of sources, including archives, print and electronic media, interviews with hunting guides, ranch owners, writers, scientists, naturalists and state and federal employees. The purpose of this compilation of facts and opinions is to provide readers with an introduction to hunting in Texas—past and present. This book is by no means the final word on hunting in Texas, nor should it be construed as such. It has always been and remains up to the individual to check with the correct governing bodies for changes in the law regarding hunting and the use of firearms.

Enjoy your hunt!

Gayne C. Young

NOTES ON WEAPONS

Countless volumes have been written about rifles and cartridges for sport hunting. Additionally, there are magazines, websites, TV shows and clubs dedicated to exploring the same subject. And yet, even with this wealth of information it seems that no consensus can be reached as to what is the absolute best caliber for a specific species.

The recommended calibers in this book were based on interviews with gunsmiths, guides, professional hunters and landowners, plus extensive research based on books, magazines and websites. The recommended calibers certainly aren't all of the calibers that could be utilized but simply the most recommended.

The three most popular suggested rounds for all big game hunting in Texas are the .270, .30-06 and 7mm. These calibers are flat shooting, hard-hitting and more than adequate for most native species. Popularity aside, no caliber can compensate for an inexperienced shooter. For this reason guides and professional hunters throughout the state, if not the world, agree that the best rifle is the rifle the hunter is most comfortable and familiar with. And there are many, many firearms out there. Hunters should find the one that works best for them.

Rifles, and especially the companies that make them, have changed considerably in the last decade or so. The old standards of *Remington, Winchester, Ruger, Browning* and *Weatherby* are facing growing competition from companies like *CZ (Ceska zbrojovka)* and *Howa*. Although the names may be unfamiliar to some hunters, these companies have a long history. The Czech company, *CZ*, for example, has been around since 1936, and their hunting rifles have been field tested and proven on the hunting grounds of Africa, Europe and Asia. I first heard of *CZ* while hunting in Africa. My PH, or professional hunter, carried a CZ chambered in .30-06. After hearing what he puts his rifle through in a year and seeing how it was still just as accurate as the day he got it, I bought one upon my return to the States. For a basic all-around hunting rifle, it's hard to beat.

Other rifle manufacturers include *Empire, Jarrett, Merkel, Kimber* and a host of others. Again, these names may not be as familiar as *Remington* or *Winchester*, but for accuracy and quality workmanship they are hard to beat.

While being comfortable with your rifle is important, it means nothing if the rifle isn't delivering the proper ammo. As a hunter and a writer, I have been subject to countless conversations, promotions and articles about bullet weight, trajectory and speed. Rather than try to understand the science, I subscribe to the practice of "go with what works." In my experience in hunting and talking to guides, I've found the *Remington Premium Safari Grade, Remington Silvertip, Winchester Fail Safe* and *Barnes X-Bullet* brand bullets to be the best.

1

TEXAS ECOLOGY, GEOGRAPHY & A BRIEF HISTORY

Encompassing more than 260,000 square miles, Texas is a land of varying and extreme geographical features. Using the criteria of elevation, soil chemistry, annual rainfall and frequency of frost-free days per year, the state can be divided into 10 very different and distinct vegetational areas.

Listed east to west, the regions of the state are:

1. Pineywoods
2. Gulf Prairies and Marshes
3. Post Oak Savannah
4. Blackland Prairies
5. Cross Timbers and Praires
6. South Texas Plains
7. Edwards Plateau
8. Rolling Plains
9. High Plains
10. Trans-Pecos

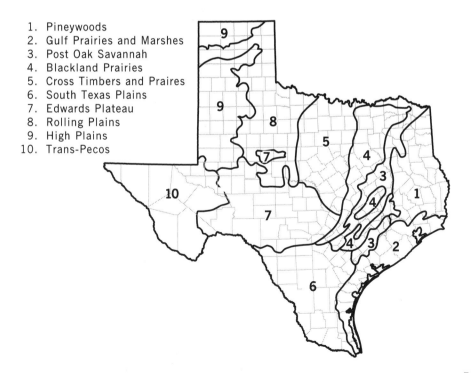

Pineywoods

Bordering the eastern state boundary of the
Sabine River, the Pineywoods of Texas covers upwards of 16 million acres and ranges in
elevation from 50 to 700 feet above sea level.
An extension of a larger forest region that
stretches from neighboring Louisiana, Okla-
homa and Arkansas, this ecological zone of Texas receives 40 to 50
inches of rain per year. Humidity and temperatures are high.

Although aptly named for the zone's dense forests of native long-
leaf, shortleaf and loblolly pines, as well as the introduced slash pine,
the area is also home to a large variety of hardwoods, including oak,
elm, hickory, magnolia, sweet gum, black gum and tupelo. The area
is also home to a wide variety of grasses and forage plants.

Completely surrounded by these forests and almost entirely within
Polk and Tyler counties is a swath of land known as the Big Thicket,
or as it is remembered by some of the older families in the area—the
bear hunters' thicket.

Having been reduced in size by human encroachment and logging, the Big Thicket now stands at about 20 miles wide and 40 miles long. Historically, this subsection of the Pineywoods was known for its dense and seemingly impenetrable vegetation and by the large numbers of bear, deer, wolves and panthers within. Today the area offers only a small glimpse of what once was.

The alteration of the Pineywoods landscape began long before the first Spanish traveled through the area in 1542. Since before A.D. 800, the Caddo Indians lived in settlements scattered throughout the East Texas area. A highly complex social group, the Caddoes lived in grass and reed-covered houses, manufactured functional and decorative ceramic pottery and farmed corn, squash, beans and sunflowers. While the Caddos were fairly stationary, except for long-distance trading with tribes as far away as what later became New Mexico, their neighbors to the south were not.

The Atakapa, "eaters of men" in Choctaw, formed loose bands that traveled extensively within the southern end of the Pineywoods and the eastern section of the Gulf Prairies and Marshes, hunting and fishing. Although the question of whether the Atakapans practiced cannibalism for subsistence or as ritual is highly debated, the level of importance that the alligator held for them is not. The Atakapans coveted alligators for their meat, their hides and their oil, used as an insect repellant.

Early Anglo settlers tended to avoid the Pineywoods or "pine barrens" as they were often referred to, preferring instead the better farmland to the west. Anglo settlers who eventually made the Pineywoods their home were generally from neighboring southern states. They found a region teaming with bears, deer, buffalo, turkey, squirrels, alligator, waterfowl and passenger pigeons.

As the Anglo population increased and Texas became an independent country, cities and towns within the Pineywoods grew dramatically. By 1837, the capital city of Houston had a population of under 2,000, a stark contrast to today's population of about 3 million.

Despite having the largest single city in Texas within its boundary, the Pineywoods is still a haven for hunters, producing great deer, feral hog, squirrel, rabbit and duck hunting.

Gulf Prairies and Marshes

The Gulf Prairies and Marshes vegetational region is a combination of coastal marshes and inland prairies of bluestem and tall grasses covering close to 10 million acres. The elevation is low, averaging 150 feet above sea level. Rainfall varies throughout the area but averages between 20 to 50 inches per year. Temperatures are warm and the humidity is high.

Although predominately grasslands, the region harbors some stands of oak, elm and other hardwoods along rivers and streams. Occasional mottes (stands or clumps of trees) of post oak, live oak and red bay also stand as "islands" among the grasses.

This coastal expanse was once home to the now extinct Karankawa Indians who migrated with the seasons between the mainland and the barrier islands. Like most nomadic, indigenous people, they

subsisted by hunting, fishing and gathering. Unlike most indigenous Texans, the Karankawa were exceptionally tall, some rumored to have been well above 6-feet, 6-inches.

Karankawan men were fierce warriors, probably in part due to their appearance. Being tall in stature, their body covered in tattoos, and with each nipple and their bottom lip pierced, they probably scared many an enemy. Also, being known as a tribe that practiced ceremonial cannibalism of their enemies probably didn't hurt either.

The Karankawa were first described in the written accounts of Álvar Núñez Cabeza de Vaca, who explored the Texas Gulf coast in 1528. Over a century later, the Karankawa were again described by the French explorer, René Robert Cavelier, Sieur de La Salle, who established a fort on the banks of Garcitas Creek near Matagorda Bay in 1685.

In the centuries following La Salle's murder by one of his own men in 1689, the coast was slowly settled by Spanish, Irish, German and other European colonists looking for a better life.

Today, like most coastal regions the world over, the Gulf Prairies and Marshes region has a number of cities and towns utilizing and enjoying life on the ocean's shore. Ranching is also a big industry in the area due to the excellent grazing provided by the prairie landscape. The area offers excellent hunting for deer, feral hog, javelina, alligator and, of course, waterfowl. Hunting for coyote, cougar, bobcat or free-range nilgai is also popular.

Post Oak Savannah

Covering roughly 7 million acres, the Post Oak Savannah or Post Oak Belt is the smallest vegetational region in Texas. Ranging in elevation from 300 to 800 feet above sea level, this region of prairie grasslands is a stark contrast to the Pineywoods region bordering it to the east. Here open meadows of Indian grass, several bluestem varieties, switch grass, and other grasses carpet the landscape. Various species of oak and other hardwoods dot the prairies and grow along rivers and bottomlands. Mesquite trees also break up the rolling grasslands of the prairies.

Rainfall averages 35 to 45 inches per year while temperatures are warm and humidity is fairly high.

The fertile soil of the open prairie and excellent growing conditions were a strong draw for early Texas settlers. The attraction of good, cheap farmland ultimately led to the forced removal of the area's original inhabitants, the Tonkawa and Wichita Indians.

In 1821, Stephen F. Austin established a colony of 300 families on land bounded by the Brazos and Colorado rivers. Despite holding all the right ingredients for successful farming ventures and the blessing of the Spanish government, the colony ran into trouble almost before it began. Mexico's independence from Spain brought about years of anxiety and feelings of uncertainty in the Texas colonies and by the end of 1835 the situation reached the boiling point.

With all signs pointing to revolution and armed conflicts against the Mexican army, Gen. Sam Houston officially designated the small town of Washington-on-the-Brazos as the headquarters of the Texas revolutionary army. In March of 1836, delegates from across what would soon become the Republic of Texas signed the Texas Declaration of Independence, wrote the Constitution of the Republic of Texas, established an interim government and designated Washington-on-the-Brazos as the Republic's first capital.

In the two centuries since the establishment of the Republic, the Post Oak Savannah saw steady growth. Although the vast herds of buffalo and deer that once roamed the savannah are long since gone, today's hunters still find ample game worth pursuing. Deer, feral hog, turkey and numerous varieties of small game offer excellent hunting as do numerous types of upland birds and waterfowl that call the savannah home.

Hunter Education Training Course

In order to legally hunt in Texas, hunters born on or after September 2, 1971, and who are at least 12 years old or older must successfully complete the state's Hunter Education Training Course. The law applies to all hunters, including those from out of state. The course averages 14 hours and covers state hunting regulations, hunting safety, outdoor skills and wildlife management and identification. Hunters can take the class over a two-day period, by a combination of an online course and one day in the field or by utilizing a home study packet and one day of field training.

For more information, hunters should contact Texas Parks and Wildlife (TPWD).

Blackland Prairies

Ranging in elevation from 300 to 500 feet above sea level, the Blackland Prairies region of Texas was once an almost endless sea of grass that held buffalo, deer, bear and mustangs by the millions. For centuries, indigenous peoples, such as the Wichita and Osage Indians, and the Anglo settlers who eventually displaced them, hunted the game of this open stretch of land for food, fat and hides. Hunting pressure was so great from Anglo encroachment that by the 1900s only a state law established to "protect and preserve" wildlife could save certain species from extinction.

As early Texans settled the prairie, they turned their sights toward farming, finding the combination of fertile soil and annual rainfall of between 30 to 40 inches per year perfect for growing cotton, wheat and sorghum.

Although called a prairie, the Blackland Prairie region contains a wide variety of timber. Oaks, pecan, elm, horse apple and the ever-encroaching mesquite grow along river and stream banks and form small wooded islands among the grasses.

Today the Blackland Prairie harbors a portion of the Dallas metroplex as well as millions of acres of cultivated farmland. Because of the population density, the resulting pollution and the suburban sprawl that surrounds the large cities, as well as the amount of already established farmland, the Blackland Prairies region is somewhat limited in hunting compared to other vegetational regions. That is not to say that there is no hunting available.

Quail, waterfowl, dove and small game hunting are popular throughout the area.

Cross Timbers and Prairies

The Cross Timbers and Prairies vegetational region consists of about 15 million acres of alternating woodlands of blackjack, shinnery, post and live oaks and prairies of Indian grass, switch grass, side oats gramma, hairy gramma and Texas winter grass. The vegeta-tion in this zone changes dramatically depending on soil composition and topography. Average rainfall is between 25 to 40 inches per year.

Having always been a haven for grazing animals, the Cross Timbers and Prairies region quickly became a Mecca for cattle ranching once settlers established a market for beef. It was here that legendary ranchers Charles Goodnight and Oliver Loving established the famous Goodnight-Loving Cattle Trail. The trail originally ran from Young County, Texas, to Las Vegas, New Mexico, where it then followed the Santa Fe Trail upward to Colorado. Taking advantage of the demand and good price for Texas beef, the trail eventually forged north to Cheyenne, Wyoming.

Originally established as an outpost to protect settlers from hostile Indians, Fort Worth soon capitalized on the cattle drives through the area and quickly became a popular hub for cowboys and the cattle industry.

Today the area is still home to cattle raising, but it's also known for its excellent turkey, dove and duck hunting. Because of the superb grazing land still available, the area also produces some of the largest deer in the state.

South Texas Plains

Known as chaparral, monte, or simply as brush country, the South Texas Plains vegetational region consists of more than 21 million acres of almost impenetrable scrub brush. Cat claw, black brush, huisache, mesquite, *guajillo* and prickly pear cactus form an ever-twisting and interlocking tapestry that conceals the once open grassland savannahs below. In some areas this subtropical dry land vegetation is so thick that hunting is only made possible by utilizing tower blinds and shooting lanes cut through the brush called *senderos*. Despite the difficulties in hunting created by the heavy foliage, this area produces some of the largest and most impressive whitetail deer in the state.

Ranging in elevation from sea level to 1,000 feet and receiving anywhere from 3 to 35 inches of rain per year, the South Texas Plains region was once a fairly open area consisting of oak and mesquite savannahs. In addition to buffalo, deer and antelope, wild mustangs and longhorn cattle roamed the savannahs in herds estimated as high as 3 million in 1835.

Sensing the market potential that the South Texas Plains could develop, Richard King and Gideon K. Lewis set up a cattle camp on Santa Gertrudis Creek in Nueces County in 1852. Although their purchase of more than 15,000 acres in 1853 certainly doesn't qualify as humble beginnings, it is meager when compared to the 825,000 acres the King Ranch owns today. What King and Lewis began more than a century and a half ago now covers more than 1,300 square miles, an area larger than the state of Rhode Island.

Today the South Texas Plains offers some of the best, and in some cases most expensive, hunting in the state. Large whitetail deer, javelina, monster feral hogs and an estimated herd of close to 30,000 free-ranging nilgai antelope beckon big game hunters. Predator hunting, dove, quail and waterfowl hunting are also top notch.

Hunting Texas' Most Dangerous Game

1852.

The distant blast of a rifle shot was followed by muffled screams for help.

Fearing the worst, the host of the hunting party spurred his horse forward into the dreadlock of South Texas scrub brush. A twisted maze of mesquite, huisache, cacti and twisted acacia pierced and sliced both rider and mount. Sweat, blood and hair rained from the frenzied gallop onto the stone dry vegetation and even drier ground. The sea of skeletal limbs and thorns suddenly opened, revealing an area of flat prairie only a few acres in size. Within the opening a cyclone of dust and turf partially concealed a chase of life and death as mounted hunters struggled to outrun a wounded, enraged bull.

Pulling his pistol and clapping his spurs, the man raced forward and into the action. The bull turned to meet the new threat and charged. He got off only a single shot before the full fury of the bull was on him. He pulled the reins tight to turn, but the bull slammed into the side of the horse at full speed.

The horse was dead on impact with one horn completely through its body, the other only partially buried in its chest after piercing through the rider's leg. Caught in a macabre moment of struggle, the bull shook its massive neck to free its horns. Each sideways lunge pulled the hole through the man's leg wider and wider.

The remainder of the hunting party rallied in rescue. Fearing that shooting the bull would only further enrage it—and jeopardize the rider's leg—the hunters decided to cut the bull's jugular vein. After much trial and error, a cut was made and the bull slowly and calmly bled to death. With time running against them, the men immediately cut through the bull's horns and pried the dead animals apart to free their friend. Only the quick actions of the hunting party and several weeks of painful bed rest saved the man's life and leg. Feeling he had been given a second chance at life, the host vowed never to hunt feral cattle again.

First brought to North America by Spanish explorers and the colonists that followed, cattle quickly adapted and flourished in the New World. But much like the horses, goats and pigs that accompanied them, cattle soon found their way into the wild through intentional release or accidental escape. Once free from human control, cattle quickly reverted to the wild nature that had supposedly been bred out of them through centuries of domestication. With few natural predators, feral cattle quickly spread throughout North America and by the 1800s they roamed the Southern and Southwestern United States by the millions. In 1835, an estimated 3 million feral cattle alone made their home on the southern plains of Texas.

Depending on the breed, the area in which they lived and the available vegetation, feral cattle could reach enormous sizes. Unchecked by man, horns grew continuously and on breeds such as longhorns, could reach a span of eight feet. Matching the animal in size was the animal's reputed tenacity if disturbed. After studying the animal in South Texas around 1874, Richard Irving Dodge wrote, "The wild bull is 'on his muscle' at all times; and though he will generally get out of the way if unmolested, the slightest provocation will convert him into a most aggressive and dangerous enemy."

Once provoked, a feral bull could prove to be as difficult to stop as a Cape buffalo, especially if less than adequate firepower was utilized. Facing a bull head-on took a great deal of bravado (or ignorance). Having heard of plenty of hunts that had gone wrong, Dodge said of bull hunters, "He knows that the chances are a thousand to one against his bringing the animal down with one shot, and that the explosion of the gun will bring the bull upon him in full charge." Such was the case with Gen. Zachary Taylor's army during the Spanish-American War.

During the army's march from Corpus Christi to Matamoras in 1846, supplies were scarce. The 150 miles between the two towns was wild, untamed and relatively free of farms and people. Seeing a longhorn bull in the distance must have seemed like a complete blessing to a young soldier with little in his stomach.

The soldier aimed and fired. Undaunted by his wound or the number of soldiers before him, the bull charged forward. Rather than reload, the young soldier turned and ran into the relative safety of the columns. The angry bull followed, scattering several regiments in its path. Despite the army's formidable reputation, the bull escaped without receiving further injury.

—*Portions of this piece first appeared in* Sporting Classics Magazine.

Edwards Plateau

Home to some of the largest deer herds in North America, the Edwards Plateau, or Hill Country, is a favorite of hunters from around the world. More than 50 percent of the white-tail deer in Texas reside in the Hill Country and hunters' success rate is often 100 percent.

In addition to a tremendous population of native deer, the area is also home to some of the largest herds of exotic species (both free ranging and high fenced) in the state. Some animals, such as aoudad, are more plentiful in the Hill Country than in their native region.

Located in the south central region of the state, this rolling-to-mountainous area encompasses about 25 million acres and ranges in elevation from 100 to 3,000 feet above sea level. The eastern portion of this vegetational zone is predominantly intermittent woodland of live oak, shinnery oak, mesquite and juniper. Cypress trees can also be found in large numbers growing along streambeds and perennial springs. Heading west, woodlands slowly give way to prairies of grazing grasses such as cane bluestem, silver bluestem, love grass, curly mesquite and buffalo.

Evidence of some of the first Texans can be found in the south-western region of the Edwards Plateau. About 12,000 years ago, early man hunted species of elephant, camel, bison and horse that roamed the lush savannahs of the time. Dramatic climate changes helped to bring about the extinction of larger game, considerable changes in plant life and the people who depended on them.

About 7,000 years ago, the game was smaller but with a landscape and climate much like today. Evidence of the culture of that period can be found in the colorfully vivid rock paintings in caves and rock overhangs such as those located at Fate Bell Shelter and Panther Cave of Seminole Canyon State Park, near Del Rio.

West of this area and several millennia later, a traveler might have stumbled on the town of Langtry, where Roy Bean declared himself not only a judge but as the only "Law West of the Pecos." Although the mystique of the legendary Judge Roy Bean conjures up the often-violent image of the western frontier, the true settling of the Edwards Plateau is far less grandiose.

As the names of many Hill Country cities—such as Fredericks-burg, Boerne and New Braunfels—suggest, a good portion of the Edwards Plateau was settled by German immigrants. The German colonization was brought about in part by Johann Friedrich Ernst who, after receiving a grant for more than 4,000 acres in 1831 in what is now Austin County, advertised the area through a series of "letters" home. Although Ernst exaggerated about the "winterless climate" of the area, he certainly didn't stretch the truth when he praised the land's excellent hunting and fishing.

What Ernst wrote more than a century and a half ago still holds true today. The Edwards Plateau has excellent hunting. Today's hunt-ers will find incredible deer and javelina hunting as well as free-rang-ing exotics such as axis, sika and fallow.

Texas Weather

Nobody but fools and newcomers predict the weather in Texas.
— Texas Saying

Much like its geography, the weather in Texas is a study in con-trasting extremes. While one portion of the state contends with torrential downpours, another is at the mercy of a year-long drought. Sleet can be blanketing the high plains of the Panhandle while people in the Lower Rio Grande Valley are running their air conditioners. And while ranchers in West Texas curse the high wind and the dust storms it brings, people along the Gulf Coast contend with humidity so high that some would argue that it's actually drizzle. Although these variances are easily attributed to the sheer size of the state, extremes occurring within the same twenty-four hour period in the same location cannot.

The old Texas adage, "If you don't like the weather, wait awhile, it'll change" couldn't be truer. What may seem like the perfect day can change in a matter of hours. In some portions of the state, even the turning of day into night can bring about a drop of thirty degrees in temperature. This variance in temperature can be even greater if a "blue norther" blows in, bringing with it polar-like conditions.

The bottom line on Texas weather is to expect the unexpected and be prepared for the worst, especially when afield.

Extremes in Texas Weather

Coldest day: -23° in Seminole on February 8, 1933

Hottest day: 120° in Monahans on June 28, 1994

Most rain in 24-hour period: 43 inches (unofficial) in Alvin on July 25, 1979

Most snowfall in 24-hour period: 24 inches in Plainview on February 3, 1956

Highest sustained winds: 145 mph during Hurricane Carla in Port Lavaca on September 11, 1961

Rolling Plains

The Rolling Plains region of Northern Texas consists of approximately 24 million acres of woodland prairie mix. Actually an extension of the Great Plains of the central United States, this area is almost evenly split between mesquite woodlands and prairies with grasses such as sand and silver bluestem, Texas winter grass and buffalo grass. Rainfall averages between 18 to 30 inches per year.

This region is the eastern most boundary of the Llano Estacado, or Staked Plains, a high mesa of approximately 32,000 square miles that continues through the High Plains vegetational region and into New Mexico. The name actually refers to the fact that the area is so flat that early Spanish explorers had to set "stakes" across the plains in order to not get lost. Known to early explorers as the Great American Desert, this flat, semi-arid region was considered to be the last stronghold of the Comanche Indians. Early settlers lived in such fear of the Comanches that they incorrectly associated the name "Staked Plains" with what the Indians would do to white settlers if captured: stake them out on the plains.

By following the buffalo, the Comanche first came to Texas from the plains of Colorado and Kansas. Finding a warmer climate, millions of buffalo and better access to mustangs, the Comanche established a wide territory, conquering anyone that got in their way. It was in Texas that the Comanche got the name that we know them by today. Originally called *Komantcia*, meaning "enemy" or "anyone who wants to fight me all the time," by the Ute Indians, the name was adopted and changed by both Spanish and American settlers.

Being nomadic hunters, the Comanche derived almost their entire existence from buffalo. Nothing of the animal was wasted. Meat,

hide, bones, fat, intestines and even their dung provided the Comanche with their very way of life. It was their dependence on buffalo that would be one of the largest factors in their ultimate defeat. Once the buffalo were nearly exterminated at the hands of the U.S. Government and others, the Comanche had less than a fighting chance at survival.

Although they no longer cover the Rolling Plains of Texas in the millions, buffalo can still be hunted today for a fee, along with many other species on private ranches. In addition to hunting on private land, plenty of opportunity exists for hunters who choose to try their luck on public land for opportunities at mule and whitetail deer, pronghorn antelope and free-ranging aoudad. Bird and waterfowl hunting is also top notch.

High Plains

Very similar in makeup to the Rolling Plains region and bordering it to the east, the High Plains vegetational region is about 19 million acres of flat, treeless expanse. Once an immense prairie, today the plains are becoming more and more dotted with intruding growths of yucca, mesquite, sagebrush and shinnery oak. Despite this intrusion, native grasses such as blue gramma, buffalo grass, bluestem, western wheatgrass and other varieties still remain throughout the region.

Shallow lakes, known as *playas*, collect and temporarily hold some of the regions annual rainfall of between 15 to 21 inches per year before it filters down into the immense underground aquifers of the region. These *playas* not only help feed the aquifers and supply fresh water for grazing animals but also attract geese and ducks during their annual migration.

Although seemingly flat, the High Plains is home to the largest canyon in the state. Palo Duro, meaning "hardwood" in Spanish,

begins 15 miles south of Amarillo in Randall County. From there the canyon snakes southeast for 60 miles, changing in elevation from 3,500 to 2,400 feet above sea level.

The history of Palo Duro is almost as long as the canyon itself. Ten thousand years ago the canyon was home to giant bison, mammoths and the prehistoric people that hunted them. Pre-horse-culture Apache Indians hunted our modern bison within and around the canyon, as did the Comanche and Kiowa three centuries later. Members of Coronado's expedition were probably the first Europeans to set eyes upon the canyon's 800-foot walls while Capt. Randolph B. Marcy was the first to officially explore the area in 1852. After the final defeat of the Comanche Indians in the canyon in 1874, the area was mapped and ready for settlement. In 1876, Charles Goodnight drove a herd of cattle into the canyon, built a crude dugout home, and established the JA Ranch.

In 1957, Texas Parks and Wildlife introduced a small number of aoudad, or Barbary sheep, in the canyon. The herd adapted better than expected and nearly 20 years later had grown to nearly 1,500. Today this herd constitutes only a small fraction of the region's free ranging game population.

Today, in addition to aoudad, the High Plains region is known for great mule and whitetail deer hunting as well as pronghorn antelope, upland game, birds and waterfowl.

Trans-Pecos Mountains and Basins

The Trans-Pecos Mountains and Basins vegetational region is what the majority of the world thinks Texas looks like. In a way they're right. This 18 million acre expanse of cactus and thorn bearing plants has often been the backdrop of Western movies and pulp cowboy novels. The landscape is sparse and desolate, dry and open. It receives as little as 8 inches of rainfall per year and sources of permanent water are extremely scarce. But this is only part of the area.

Ranging in elevation from 2,500 to 8,751 feet above sea level, the region also has the state's highest (and only) peaks. The grass-covered mountains are home to forests of piñon and ponderosa pine as well as juniper. These oases of cooler temperatures and green vegetation are a stark contrast to the Chihuahuan Desert that surrounds them.

The Trans-Pecos is truly a land of extremes. Within its boundaries are the state's highest mountains and the nation's largest desert. Counties as large as Connecticut and Rhode Island combined hold populations of barely 9,000 people. It is a land that many cultures tried to claim but none really controlled.

Because of these extremes, this area offers some of the most adventurous hunting in the state. Hunters entering the region unprepared can face any number of unforeseen hardships and dangers. If nothing else, the Trans-Pecos is unforgiving.

Although the elk and bear that once thrived in great numbers and roamed throughout the region have dwindled in number, many other game animals are still available. Antelope, mule and whitetail deer, free-ranging aoudad and javelina offer hunters plenty of opportunity. Turkey, quail and dove hunting are also extremely popular. Hunters who seek dangerous game flock to the area to try their luck at cougar hunting.

2

Big Game

I asked him [Juan Brebel] also what animals were found in the great prairies. He told me that from the Rio Azul upwards, on both sides of the Red River, there were innumerable quantities of wild horses, buffaloes or bison, bears, wolves, elk, deer, foxes, javalines, or wild hogs, fallow deer, wild goats, white hares, rabbits, etc.

— John Sibley, 1765

I need not say that in variety, quantity, and quality of game, the Texas country exceeds Scotland, to say nothing of the climate.

— Captain Flack, 1866

Texas is blessed with an abundance of game animals. Some species, such as the whitetail deer, are more plentiful in Texas than anywhere else in the United States while others, such as big horn sheep, are fairly rare. Due to shifting attitudes pertaining to sound conservation through managed land and managed game, hunting may be better today than it has ever been. Although the days of hunting expeditions slowly meandering throughout the state's endless landscape are gone, hunters can still hunt tracts of public and private land consisting of tens of thousands of acres with no interior fences. The landscape hunted may be smaller, but the opportunities are not.

Big Horn Sheep
Ovis Canadensis

> *As I was riding in advance of the caravan, I saw three moun-*
> *tain-sheep, one of which I might have killed if I had ventured*
> *to follow them; but, at a distance, I mistook the animals for*
> *bears, and confess that I had no desire to encounter three of*
> *these beasts alone. When I discovered my error they were too*
> *high up between the rocks.*
>
> —Julius Frobel, Texas, 1854

Whether or not big horn sheep are a native or reintroduced species is a matter of personal interpretation. Once roaming throughout
Trans-Pecos Texas, big horn numbers were pushed to the brink of
extinction by human encroachment and the introduction of domestic
sheep. Despite full protection under the law, numbers continued to
decrease until 1959 when only 14 native animals were known to exist. Today's animals are the result of several different and successful
restocking efforts begun in 1973. In 2004, nearly 700 big horn sheep
roamed the mountains of West Texas.

More correctly identified as mountain sheep, the big horn is an extremely wary and difficult game animal to hunt. Inhabiting only the rough, rock-strewn mountainous terrain of the Trans-Pecos region, big horn prefer to graze on wide open and sparsely vegetated bluffs and sheer slopes. This allows them plenty of opportunity for a quick escape once danger is spotted.

True to their goat-like nature, big horn eat things other animals wouldn't attempt to swallow. In Texas, they feed on ocotillo, sotol, prickly pear, yucca, wild onions and penstemon. These and the other succulents that make up their diet provide them with most, if not all, of their water needs.

Big horns are massive animals, standing as much as 36 inches tall at the shoulder and weighing upwards of 300 pounds (perhaps this is the reason Julius Frobel mistook them for bears at a distance), although most average between 150 and 170 pounds. Both sexes carry horns, with those of the male being considerably larger and thicker than the females. Horns grow back, curling close to the head before jutting off at eye level. These "big horns" sometimes appear grossly out of proportion to an animal's body. Exceptional trophies may be 43 inches in length and up to 16 inches in circumference at the base. Both sexes are brownish to tan with a distinct white rump patch divided by a dark, vertical tail stripe.

Few hunters are aware of how large big horns are until they are viewed close up, which is a very unlikely event given the sheep's incredible eyesight. Hunting big horn is traditionally done by spot and stalk and getting within easy shooting distance of a trophy ram is almost unheard of.

Due to the small number of big horn in the state, hunting is by permit only. Landowners are given permits from the state, and they in turn sell the right to hunt, usually for an extremely hefty fee. Another method of obtaining a permit is by lottery drawing through Texas Parks and Wildlife. If drawn, state biologists guide hunters on state management areas.

Grand slam 1999

Best places to hunt: Big horn sheep live only in the Trans-Pecos Mountains and Basins region of the state. Permits from landowners are extremely difficult to come by and can cost more than $150,000. A better bet fiscally—although still a long shot odds wise—is to attempt to be drawn for a hunt on a Texas Wildlife Management Area through Texas Parks and Wildlife.

Recommended calibers: Due to the big horn's size and the distance of most shots, nothing under a 30 caliber is recommended. Best bets are .30-06, 7mm or 300 Mag. The newer WSM calibers are also considered a safe bet.

Texas Blinds

In Texas, the word "blind" is an all-encompassing term that refers to anything from a completely enclosed structure with insulation, glass windows and gas heater to a folding chair strategically placed behind some brush. As one of the more popular hunting methods in Texas, blinds run the gamut of size, structure and cost. A blind can be homemade or commercially manufactured, elevated or half buried in the ground, painted camouflage to match the landscape or painted faint blue to resemble the sky. About the only thing Texas blinds have in common is that they are all a place to lie in wait for game.

Portable blinds are growing in popularity because they allow easy setup and movement between locations. These can be an elevated tripod with an attached swivel chair, a tree stand that is set into place and chained against a tree or one of the newer "pop up" blinds made from fiberglass poles and synthetic material similar to that used on tents. Portable blinds are commonly used by bow hunters who have to move frequently because of game movement and by those hunting on public lands.

Far more comfortable are the fully enclosed, permanent blinds. These can be either homemade or commercially manufactured. Homemade varieties tend to be constructed from plywood or similar material. Although some have either glass or Plexiglas windows, others have

Tower blind from Younger Bros. Deer Blinds.

nothing but an open space to shoot through. Fancier blinds have insulation, carpet, shelves, gun racks, comfy chairs and portable heaters. Elevated stands have either a ladder or stairs.

Manufactured blinds come in a variety of sizes, heights and finishes. They can accommodate one hunter, two or more, or someone in need of handicap access. Some offer insulation, tinted windows, manually operated air vents and built-in shelves. Fabricated blinds are popular in Texas and there are dozens of companies competing for hunters' business. Much like homemade blinds, the only factor in what a blind will or won't have is strictly financial.

Collared Peccary
Tayassu tajacu

> *Bears are very plenty, but we are obliged to use great care when hunting for them, lest the havalenas kill our dogs.*
> — W. B. Dewees, 1822

> *The most formidable animal, and one to be most dreaded is the Mexican hog. They have a grown one in a pen here. It is about the size of a half grown hog. Its back is covered with hair resembling porcupine quills, but much finer. It has enormous teeth & they come together like sheers & cut every thing in pieces.*
> — A. J. Pickett, 1856

Having a legendary reputation as being a tenacious, bloodthirsty juggernaut, the collared peccary is undoubtedly the most misunderstood game animal in Texas. Generally referred to as javelinas or Mexican hogs, peccaries once ranged as far north as the Red River and as far east as the Brazos Valley. Pressure from livestock, encroachment by man, the conversion of land to agricultural usage, as well as the com-

mercial hunting of the animal for its hide prior to 1939 pushed the peccary to its current range of the Trans-Pecos region and the South Texas Plains.

Collared peccaries are small animals, ranging in weight from 25 to upwards of 60 pounds and standing 20 to 24 inches tall at the shoulder. They are covered with a thick, bristled hide that was once commercially harvested for leather, paint brushes and shaving brushes. Buried within this thick hide, just above the rump, is a small musk gland thought to be used to mark territories and communicate with others within the herd. Peccaries are extremely social animals, traveling in herds of anywhere from 10 to 50 animals.

Peccaries can go up to a week without drinking water, gathering most of their fluid needs from cactus and other plants in their diet. They are generally herbivores but occasionally eat insects or other small animals. Unlike the animal they are often confused for, peccaries do not root for food, as do hogs. Rather they push around the surface searching for anything edible.

The peccary's dagger-like tusks that connect in a scissor fashion no doubt enhance their fearsome reputation. Used in self-defense if cornered or pushed, their tusks can slice open a dog or hunter in a

Author Gayne Young with a javelina taken near Pearsall.

matter of seconds. They also chatter their teeth in rapid succession, sounding similar to castanets, when agitated or alarmed. This sound, when combined with the animal's extremely poor vision makes for rampant confusion and undoubtedly has only helped to fuel stories of charging when disturbed by humans.

Best places to hunt: Collared peccary are found in the South Texas Plains and Trans-Pecos Mountains and Basins regions of the state. Smaller numbers can occasionally be found in the southern Edwards Plateau region as well.

Recommended calibers: Despite their exaggerated temperament, javelinas are fairly small. Although calibers such as .223 and .22-250 are more than adequate, many hunters take javelinas with the same rifle they use on whitetails.

Roosevelt's Javelina

The weather was especially hot and dry in the area surrounding the Frio River in April 1892. Long stretches of river had dried to nothing more than coarse gravel beds and the sections of riverbed that did hold water contained few, if any, fish. Even the shade from the numerous cypress, live oak and pecans along the river seemed void of life. Only the distant and occasional songs of mockingbird hinted at something stirring. For two days Uvalde rancher John Moore and a future president of the United States, Theodore Roosevelt, rode the banks of this desolate country in an unsuccessful search for javelina. By dinner of the second night, Roosevelt's disappointment in not having seen the animal he had come so far for was apparent. Sensing his anxiety, Moore and his ranch hands decided to have some fun with Roosevelt by baiting him with stories at dinner.

Moore began by telling about a time when on horseback that he and a friend were ". . . attacked in sheer wantonness by a drove of these wild little hogs." Infuriated by their disturbance, the javelinas rushed the horses in a clamoring storm of bristled hides and sharp tusks. The men fought to stay mounted as the horses reared and spun wildly. Moore pulled his revolver and fired into the angry mob. His friend immediately followed. Even with two animals down the mob continued their barrage. Spurring their horses forward the two men tried to outrun the herd but were chased for three to four hundred yards.

The next story involved the ranch's bookkeeper. Walking a narrow trail to a watering hole about a quarter mile from the ranch house, the bookkeeper suddenly found himself face to face with a javelina. Without a moment's hesitation the animal aggressively charged. With thick chaparral to either side of him, the bookkeeper turned and ran, only reaching safety by scrambling up a mesquite tree at the last second. It was there that he stayed for more than two hours while the animal stubbornly gnawed at the tree and jumped up in an attempt to reach his prey.

With a night full of stories swimming in his head, Roosevelt retired to the ranch house more eager than ever to hunt javelina.

The next morning Moore suggested that he and Roosevelt travel to an area on the Nueces River, some 30 miles south, where javelina were more plentiful. Roosevelt wholeheartedly agreed.

The trip took close to seven hours by horse, but Roosevelt enjoyed the journey. Traveling cross-country the men spotted large numbers of sandhill cranes feeding in open fields so thick with bluebonnet flowers that Roosevelt thought it the river at a distance. Huge flocks of geese flew above, their honks seemingly baiting the wild turkeys hidden among the islands of trees to call back in return. Deer tracks dotted the ground and freshly rubbed trees gave signs of large bucks.

By late afternoon, they reached the banks of the Nueces River. Much like the Frio, the Nueces was nothing more than a collection of scattered, deep pools of water, some of which were so stagnant and filled with decomposing debris that Roosevelt described them as "malarial-looking." As the day went on and travel progressed, the river eventually turned into a "semi-tropical" paradise. Great blue herons stood perfectly still waiting for the next fish to swim within striking distance and flocks of white ibis skimmed over the wide, clear waters when bothered or threatened. Deep thickets of pecan and live oaks, some covered in long tufts of grayish green moss, bordered the river on both sides. Signs of deer and turkey were plentiful as were the countless songs of birds from neighboring vegetation.

Traveling through such beauty, time sped quickly and it wasn't long before Moore and Roosevelt met a local ranch owner who was more than eager to give them information. The rancher said that a javelina had been shot in the area two or three days before and finding more shouldn't be too much trouble. This was good news for Roosevelt, who had allotted only a few days to hunt.

After further discussion, the rancher's son offered to guide

Moore and Roosevelt. He supplied the hunting party with fresh horses and a pack of dogs. Although the new guide had plenty of confidence in his dogs, he admitted that he had lent his best hunting dog to a Mexican goat-herder who lived some five miles away. If they wanted the best javelina dog in the area, they'd have to retrieve him in the morning. The decision having been made, all involved left early the next morning.

At dawn they rode south, again skirting the river, to the goat-herder's home. This stretch of river proved more beautiful than the section Moore and Roosevelt had seen the day before. The normally shallow river gave way to deep pools of huge lilies and even larger alligator gar. Numerous species of birds darted in and out of thick stands of huge pecans. It was deep within one of these massive clumps of pecans that they found the goat-herder's home.

Although the man they'd come to see wasn't at home, the hunting party was more than welcomed by the goat-herder's wife. Noting the time of their arrival, she insisted on feeding them a huge meal of goat meat and *pan de maíz* (cornbread). As the men ate, they made notice of several cured hides tacked to the wall of the sparse hut in which the herder and his wife lived. The numerous raccoon, wildcat and ring-tailed tree-civet hides only furthered the rancher's son's boast that the herder was extremely fond of hunting. By meal's end, the herder and the much wanted dog had yet to return. The goat-herder's wife said she believed her husband was out hunting and that if the men rode the surrounding area they were sure to find him. Still wanting the dog they'd come for, the men mounted up and rode on. Within a few hours they had found the herder, retrieved the rancher's son's dog and begun making their way to an area high above the river where the javelina hunting was said to be best.

Away from the river, the topography changed dramatically. Thick thorn-covered mesquite was clumped along with prickly pear as high as a man's head when mounted on horseback. Spanish bayonets and numerous species of cacti littered the ground, covering it like a carpet. It seemed as though everything except the soil itself was covered in thorns or briars. The vegetation was so bad that after following several false trails that the dogs had excitedly chased, the men had to take time out to remove clumps of thorns from their hands, arms and legs.

After a discouraging afternoon, the men had all but given up hope when five javelina were suddenly spotted in a small opening in the mesquite. The dogs lunged forward in pursuit. At the first sighting, the men spurred their mounts ahead. Moore was almost on top of a javelina when his horse winced in pain. He turned to see a sow ambling in and out of his horse's legs, slashing and biting. Seeing his friend in trouble, Roosevelt jumped from his horse, shouldered his rifle and fired. The sow dropped flat, its spine completely severed.

His horse free from danger, Moore spurred after the javelina he'd been forced to cease chasing moments earlier. Roosevelt immediately remounted and followed. The men sped forward, following a narrow trail through a maze of thorns. The javelina were waiting on them. Having reached the end of the trail, the javelina turned to charge. Moore pulled his rifle from its scabbard and pulled off a quick shot. Shot in mid-charge the animal plowed into the earth and fell over dead.

Hearing some of the dogs howl in the distance, Roosevelt turned to chase down the commotion. He dug his heels deep into his horse's flanks, pushing harder and harder in an attempt to beat the fading light. Riding into a small opening of short grass and cactus, Roosevelt came upon three dogs and a large boar flailing violently in a tangled mess. The sounds of commotion jumped in pitch as the boar ripped into one of the dogs, its tusks cutting through flesh with the speed of "castanets." Roosevelt rode into the middle of the terror and shot straight down into the boar, killing it instantly with a shot through its backbone.

That night Roosevelt relived his hunt over and over, telling and retelling his feat of taking two javelina. He said he loved the hunt and enjoyed his entire stay in Texas but couldn't help but wonder if the hunt would be more thrilling if he had used a spear rather than a rifle.

—Portions of this piece first appeared in True West Magazine

DEER

Mule Deer or Desert Mule Deer
Odocoileus hemionus crooki

Referred to as black-tail deer, mountain deer or mulies by early Anglos, mule deer have the distinction of being the game animal with the least amount of reduction in range since the time of early exploration. In fact, due to reintroduction and stricter game laws, mule deer may actually have a larger range than they once had.

Confined to the Trans-Pecos and the western high plains of the Panhandle, mule deer are large, with a mature buck weighing more than 220 pounds. Mule deer are brownish gray with a white throat patch and white rump. Their coat may turn reddish in summer. The tail is pendant shaped and tucks under during escape.

Mule deer in velvet.

Unlike whitetail deer, mule deer have dichotomously branched antlers, meaning antlers split into even forks rather than forming tines off of one main beam. Antlers divide evenly at the first fork and each branch divides again. A single brow tine is common.

Mule deer are social animals, often traveling in herds of up to 30 animals strong. On the rare occasion when mule and white-tailed deer breed, the offspring usually takes on more of the whitetail's characteristics.

Mule deer have excellent hearing as well as phenomenal eyesight. In spite of these gifts, mules detect most danger through their acute sense of smell.

When frightened or alerted to trouble, mule deer make a hasty escape by bouncing away in pogo-stick fashion. Although no one knows for sure why mule deer bounce, it is known that they can cover distances of up to 23 feet in a single bound. The distance is even greater when the deer are traveling downhill. Bounds of more than 28 feet have been measured on as little as a 7 percent slope.

In lower elevations, mule deer prefer open, arid areas covered with sagebrush, juniper, pine and bitter brush. In the mountainous Trans-Pecos region, they prefer rocky slopes dotted with lechuguilla and sotol. Because of this landscape, most, if not all, mule deer hunting is by spot and stalk. Hours are spent glassing an area for the tall racks of a mature buck with the hopes of approaching close enough for a decent shot. Regardless of how good the stalk, most hunters only get close enough to see their potential trophy bouncing off into the distance at the last second.

Best places to hunt: Mule deer are found in the Rolling Plains and High Plains regions of the state as well as the Trans-Pecos Mountains and Basins.

Recommended calibers: As all share the same habitat and are similar in size, the same calibers recommended for big horn sheep and aoudad are also good choices for mule deer. Best bets are .25-06, .270, .30-06, 7mm or 300 Mag.

What Drives Texans

In a state where the best-selling vehicle is a truck, custom built, off-road vehicles designed specifically for hunting are a serious, and big, business. There are probably more specially outfitted hunting vehicles in Texas than there are in Africa and Australia combined. Although hunting from a vehicle on public land or from a public road is illegal, hunting from one on privately held land is not. Whether hunting from open vehicles is ethical or not is a matter of personal opinion, and there are good arguments on both sides of the issue. What's not debatable is the fact that some land in Texas can't be explored in any vehicle without four-wheel drive and the right modifications.

Hunting vehicles come in all shapes, sizes, configurations and prices. At the low end of prices are the extremely worn and well-used "lease" or "ranch" trucks. These basic trucks and 4x4s vary in model, year and amount of rust and Bondo, but all serve as the basic mode of transportation on private land during hunting season. The only requirements seem to be that the vehicle is equipped with four-wheel drive, can accommodate hunters, game, and all the feed, tools and other necessities needed for running a successful hunting operation.

Far removed from these basic model runarounds are the custom built or aftermarket safari vehicles employed by large hunting ranches and affluent sportsmen. Equipped with brush guards, winches, gun racks, lights, elevated seats, roll bars and a multitude of other extras, these vehicles are often designed and built on already fully loaded trucks and SUVs. Custom garages that cater only to the hunting vehicle market have sprung up across the state, some exclusively dealing with only one specific make of vehicle. Most shops have a fairly long waiting list.

One of the better and more well-known garages is *What-a-Jeep* in Amarillo. The owners design, modify and build upon any year model 97 and above Jeep Wrangler. One of the more popular conversions *What-a-Jeep* offers is the "stretch," which turns the normally two-door model into a four-door model. After the initial conversion, clients often add brush guards, winches, bikini tops, custom interior, gun racks, swivel lights and shooting benches. As owner Mitch Hutchens puts it, "We can do just about anything a client can dream of. And often have."

Somewhere in-between these two levels of extravagance lie the so called "off road utility vehicles." These golf cart-sized vehicles from manufacturers such as *Yamaha*, *Kawasaki* and *Gator* are available with all the bells and whistles of their larger truck cousins. Most have four-wheel drive, gun racks and some sort of cargo space. Options include everything from diesel engines to camouflage paint.

Below off-road utility vehicles in size but far exceeding them in noise levels are All Terrain Vehicles or ATVs. These small, four-wheel drive vehicles are straddled like a motorcycle and controlled with handlebars. They are able to go places larger vehicles can't and can even be fitted with trailers, luggage racks and a winch. ATVs are allowed on some public land for transportation purposes only.

Although not near as many as there used to be, some hunters still opt for the original Texas hunting vehicle: the horse.

Whitetail Deer or Texas White-tailed Deer
Odocoileus virginianus

During the remainder of the day we passed through a flat country and found a great many deer. We saw around us, almost at the same time, as many as three or four hundred of these animals.

— Juan Antonio de la Peña, 1722

The deer are so numerous, that they are often found in herds of several thousands...

— Francis Moore, Jr., 1840

Deer of about the size of our largest fallow deer, and in herds of from ten to a thousand, are common in every part of the country.

— Arthur Ikin, 1841

Although the sight of whitetail deer (correctly identified as white-tailed deer) in herds of upwards to a thousand in number may seem difficult to believe, many early settlers and explorers in Texas, even as far back as the 1700s, made reference to such tremendous herds in diaries, journals and letters home. In some portions of the (future) state, whitetail herds were larger than buffalo, an animal that few people have trouble in accepting as gathering in herds that large.

To these early Anglo settlers and the indigenous people that came and lived before them, the deer was easily accessible food. So accessible, in fact, that by as early as 1840 settlers began to notice a severe drop in whitetail numbers. Only a minute portion of this tremendous decline can be attributed to subsistence hunting. The larger impact came from land encroachment, competition from newly introduced livestock and, just as with the buffalo, senseless and unjustified slaughter. The extent of this slaughter is well described by John C. Reid, who wrote in 1857:

"Various modes are adopted, by the citizens here, for killing the wild animal. Game is ever in season. Thousands of deer are slain by the light of the fire pan; by snares and pitfalls, by the laying concealed near holes of water or "licks"; stooping in the tall grass and attracting those in sight by occasionally tossing in the air an unfurled red handkerchief; or shooting those gentle enough to allow you to approach. They are often beguiled by the docility of others already domesticated; by driving them towards standers in waiting; by chasing upon fleet horses and lassoing them."

While these methods are almost inconceivable to sportsmen today, the numbers by which deer were slaughtered is almost incomprehensible. Although there was no official census taken in the years during Anglo settlement, it is estimated that there could have been between 30 million to 125 million deer roaming the land that would become Texas. By 1900, it was estimated that there were only 500,000 deer in the entire *United States*. Like the buffalo, deer were slaughtered almost to the point of no return.

With government intervention and the establishment of strict game laws, deer rebounded quickly. By 1990, the number of deer in Texas had reached between 3 and 4 million. Just how well deer rebounded is made apparent when considering that the average number of deer legally taken in the state is close to what the deer population

Bushlan pro-hunter Robbie Carter with a mature whitetail.

of the entire country was in 1900. In fact, in some areas of the state deer are actually dangerously overpopulated.

Today deer hunting in Texas is not only well regulated but also a big business. How big? Consider that in 2004 a group of Texas investors near Seguin paid $450,000 for a massively racked buck that they planned to breed for profit. By taking orders for semen at $3,500 and bred does at $25,000, the investment group expected to recoup their money almost before they began. At the hunting end of the spectrum, the amount of money involved is almost as astronomical. Hunts for high-scoring Boone and Crockett Club whitetails in the South Texas region alone have gone in excess of $20,000. Despite this monetary excess, plenty of deer hunting exists for individuals with tighter budgets.

What whitetails eat is partially determined by where they live. In the Edwards Plateau region, for example, deer graze twice as much as they browse. More than 67 percent of their feeding time is spent eating grasses and forbs. In South Texas, the numbers are almost reversed. Deer browse twice as much as they graze. Percentages and diet are altered considerably when supplemental feeding and land management are entered into the equation.

Just as with their diet, whitetail weight is heavily determined by where deer live. Deer in the eastern portion of the state and in the Edwards Plateau tend to be smaller in body than those in South Texas or on the upper plains. In general though, whitetail average from between 70 to 150 pounds.

In terms of color, whitetails are grayish brown or grayish blue. Coats take on a reddish brown tinge in winter. The under parts are lighter in color, if not white. True to their name, whitetails have a white tail that stands erect when fleeing danger. Antlers grow outward from the back of the head before curving slightly forward. Each tine grows off of a main beam.

There are probably as many hunting methods for deer as there are hunters, but in Texas, hunting from an elevated stand is by far the most common. Whether as simple as a tripod or tree stand, or as lavish as an enclosed box blind with insulated walls and sliding windows, elevated blinds offer better visibility and, theoretically, more opportunities at game. Elevated blinds also offer the best possibilities to see wildlife often overlooked or unseen while hunting from the ground.

Whitetail in velvet.

Although a hotly debated subject, many elevated stands overlook a feeder or other food source. Some hunters find the idea of shooting an animal over deposited food unethical and immoral. Others find that it allows the hunter more time to judge the animal as well as add to the probability of making a clean shot. Regardless of the views taken, hunting deer over feeders is not illegal in Texas.

During the rut many hunters take to "rattling," the act of bashing and scraping antlers together to imitate the sound of sparing bucks. This and other "calling" techniques add an element of excitement to the hunt most often not associated with pursuing deer. Rattling is sometimes a simple addition to the more traditional spot-and-stalk method of hunting.

In Texas, deer may be hunted with almost any type of weapon. Hunters have their choice between muzzleloaders, traditional firearms (center fire only), archery and handgun.

Best places to hunt: Anywhere. Whitetails are found in great numbers throughout the state. The largest bucks tend to come from the South Texas Plains region. Deer in the Rolling Plains, High Plains and Trans-Pecos Mountains and Basins regions come in a close second. The eastern regions as well as the Edwards Plateau generally hold much smaller animals.

Recommended calibers: In the eastern and central portions of the state, calibers such as .270 or .30-06 are fairly common. Many hunters have turned to the newer 12 or 20 gauge slug guns with great success, especially in the thicker Pineywoods region. Some hunters swear by .222, .223, or .243 for smaller deer. For the remainder of the state anything from a .270 and up (within reason) is more than sufficient.

The Rut

Rut
1 : an annually recurrent state of sexual excitement in the male deer; broadly: sexual excitement in a mammal especially when periodic
2 : the period during which rut normally occurs—often used with "the"

— Merriam-Webster Online

Simply put, the rut is the period in which deer breed. And while all ungulates with antlers experience a period of rut, in Texas the term is generally used only in association with whitetail deer (as a

Well-used Whitetail Rub

rule Texans leave other species to breed unmolested). During this period of sexual drive, whitetail bucks are at their most vulnerable. They tend to be more active and less cautious—traits that hunters anxiously look forward to taking advantage of each year. Bucks are also more vocal, often announcing their presence with low grunts and more than willing to fight for a mate. It is this eagerness to accept a challenge for breeding rights that makes "rattling" such a successful hunt method.

In Texas, the rut generally occurs for several weeks in November and December. Bucks in some areas enter the rut as early as the end of August or as late as mid-November. For the latest, up-to-date information on the rut, hunters should contact Texas Parks and Wildlife. Regardless of when the hunt begins, many hunters feel it's the most exciting time to hunt.

Pronghorn
Antilocapra Americana

*This day, for the first time, we saw an animal somewhat
resembling both the deer and the goat, but with flesh preferable
to that of either.... It runs with great speed, and has a stride
like a horse. How fast the animal can run when in possession of
four legs is a question I am at a loss to answer, but one with a
fore leg broken by a rifle ball made out to escape from one of our
best horses after a long chase.*

— George Kendall, 1844

*Here I first saw the antelope. We saw several herds of half a
dozen or more. The escort tried to get a shot at them in vain.
Their flight is the poetry of motion. They trot and gallop and
sometimes seem to skim along the prairie like birds...*

— William Preston Johnston, 1855

The pronghorn is now restricted to the Trans-Pecos and Panhandle
regions of the state, but it once ranged freely over the western two-
thirds of the state in herds early explorers found too large to esti-
mate in size. Despite being one of the more desirable game animals

in the state and numerous conservation efforts, pronghorn have not rebounded as quickly as other animals once teetering on the edge of extinction, such as buffalo, deer and alligator. In 1990, the statewide population only hovered around 14,000. Because of these relatively low numbers, pronghorn hunting is only allowed through landowners with state-obtained permits.

Although commonly referred to as the pronghorn antelope, *Antilocapra Americana* is neither an antelope nor a sheep. Rather it is the sole-surviving member of the family Antilocapridae, a group of prehistoric animals that by definition means "only the pronghorn." This group has split horns made of a hair-like substance that grows around a bony core. Pronghorns are not only the only animals to have split horns but are also the only ones to actually shed them as well.

Outfitter Wes Hughes (left) and guide E. J. Varos with a trophy West Texas antelope.

Pronghorn are truly adapted to life on the open plains. They have large eyes and almost telescopic vision. When threatened or hard pressed they can flee at speeds of more than 40 miles per hour, making them the fastest animal on the North American continent. They graze on plants that are poisonous to domesticated sheep and goats and are able to go long periods without water.

Much is made of the pronghorn's unwillingness to jump even the smallest of obstructions. Although pronghorn can jump fences or any other reasonable obstacle, more times than not they choose not to. Why isn't exactly known. It certainly isn't because of their size. Pronghorns on average are smaller than whitetails. However, large males can reach upwards of 130 pounds.

Due to the wide-open spaces they inhabit, pronghorn hunting generally requires long-distance shots. Shorter distances can be obtained by utilizing blinds, staking out water holes or by using decoys.

Another method of hunting takes advantage of the animal's strong sense of curiosity. Extremely inquisitive, pronghorn will often approach a moving object such as a waved handkerchief to further investigate. Although a popular method of attracting animals, spot and stalk is generally the name of the game when it comes to pronghorn hunting.

Best places to hunt: Pronghorn are restricted to the High Plains, Rolling Plains and Trans-Pecos Mountains and Basins regions of the state. Permits for pronghorn are available through landowners or their outfitters as well as through Texas Parks and Wildlife via public hunting lottery.

Recommended calibers: Pronghorn are not very large body-wise, but shots are often at long distances. Flat shooting calibers such as .25-06, .270, .270 Winchester Mag., .300 Winchester Mag. or higher are good bets.

After the Shot

To the horror of many hunters, not every shot immediately drops an animal. Sometimes a wounded animal runs a fair distance before dropping. Other times, what looked like a sure hit turned out to be a narrow miss. Situations such as these often leave hunters with feelings of self-doubt, aggravation and frustration. But the best thing a hunter can do when there is doubt about whether an animal was hit is to sit quietly and think through the shot.

The following suggestions apply to deer and deer-sized game.

Think about what you heard.
Did you hear the impact of the bullet or arrow?
Did you hear the animal crash after it ran off?
Did you hear it bellow?

Think about what the animal did.

Did the animal fall down, jump up or hunch over before running off?

If none of the above happened, then the animal probably wasn't hit. If any of the above happened, then the animal was hit—the only questions now are how badly was it hit and where did it go?

Tracking a wounded animal.

Give the animal time to succumb to its wounds: between 20 and 30 minutes.

Note where the animal was when it was shot.

Investigate the area for blood or other signs such as hair or bone that may indicate a hit:

- Dark blood indicates a hit to the heart, liver or kidney.
- Bright red usually indicates a hit to the muscle.
- Pink or light red, frothy blood indicates a lung hit.
- Splatter indicates a major hit to an artery or heart.
- Watery blood, mixed with stomach fluids or contents indicates a "gut shot."

Utilizing tracks, a blood trail and your knowledge of which direction the animal ran, follow the trail the best you can until the animal is found.

Other tips

Remember to scan ahead of you for the animal or animal movement as you trail.

Stay off of the animal's trail. You might have to utilize it again.

If the trail goes cold, try it again or circle the area in search of the animal.

Two hunters searching for a downed animal is always better than one.

Watch for buzzards.

If you're sure the animal was hit, don't give up.

FREE RANGE EXOTICS

Whether knowingly released into the wild or through accidental escape, Texas is home to a growing number of exotic, or non-indigenous, animals. In some cases there are more of an animal species in Texas than in the animal's own native country. Free-range exotics are not treated as game animals under the law, so they can be hunted at anytime during the year so long as the landowner's permission is obtained. Almost all of these exotics are available behind high fences, as well—for a hefty price.

Aoudad
Ammotragus lervia

Originally released into the Palo Duro Canyon area by Texas Parks and Wildlife in an effort to establish more hunting opportunities, aoudad, or Barbary sheep, are one of the more prolific species of exotics in the state. A native of the Barbary Coast of Northern Africa, aoudads adapted easily to the harsh, arid, almost vertical conditions of Palo Duro Canyon. Because of this original herd and the unintentional escape of privately held herds elsewhere, aoudads now range throughout almost every part of the state except the eastern Pineywoods.

Aoudads, one of the largest exotics in Texas, measure almost 4 feet tall at the shoulder and weigh upwards of 300 pounds. They are reddish brown with a long fringe of hair running the length of their neck to lower chest. Their horns are composed of a series of raised rings that sweep outward before curling back inward toward the head. Male's horns grow together at the base over time.

Hunter and owner of Sportsmen on Film, Ken Wilson,
with a large, free-ranging aoudad.

Aoudads are social animals that travel and feed in large herds. On some large ranches in the Hill Country and in the Davis Mountains, herds of more than 100 animals have been observed. These numbers, when combined with the animal's superior eyesight, make the aoudad an extremely difficult animal to hunt.

Best places to hunt: Free-ranging aoudad occur in the Rolling Plains, High Plains, South Texas Plains, and Trans-Pecos Mountains and Basins regions of the state. Aoudad can also be found on game ranches throughout the state.

Recommended calibers: With good-sized animals pushing 300 pounds, nothing under .30 caliber is recommended. Best bets are .30-06, 7mm, or 300 Mag.

Axis
Cervus axix

Called chital deer or spotted deer in their native India, axis deer are the most numerous exotic deer in the state. They are reddish brown with white spots, closely resembling whitetail fawns. They are predominately grazers but occasionally browse on such foliage as live oak and sumac.

Axis are typically larger than whitetail, standing nearly 3 feet at the shoulder with mature bucks weighing in excess of 160 pounds. Their antlers have three tines with the brow tine growing at a right angle to the rest.

Anatomically and vocally, axis are more closely compared to elk than whitetail. Both sexes have barking calls and males have a bugle-like cry during the rut. Axis are social animals that travel in groups as large as a hundred although smaller herds are more common.

Axis are hunted in a number of ways. On most game ranches, safari style spot and stalk is generally the norm. Hunting from an elevated stand is also popular.

Best places to hunt: Free-ranging axis are found almost everywhere in the state although the largest populations are in the Edwards Plateau region. Large numbers are also found in the South Texas Plains region. Axis are probably the most numerous exotic found on game ranches.

Recommended calibers: Any larger caliber deer rifle such as the .270, .30-06 or 7mm are a good choice. However, many hunters have been dumbstruck upon witnessing the axis they downed with a .30-06 get up and run away. Axis deer are much tougher than they appear and caution must be taken to avoid wounding an animal, thus leaving hunters with nothing left to show for it except a high trophy fee.

Hunter Joel O'Shoney with a typical free-ranging axis deer taken near Kerrville.

Blackbuck Antelope
Antilope cervicapra

A native of India and Pakistan, blackbuck antelope were among the first introduced species to the state, with the first animals reaching the Edwards Plateau in 1932. Seventy-plus years later 80 percent of all free-range blackbuck antelope still reside in the Edwards Plateau region. This isolated pocket is due in part to the animal's intolerance for the colder temperatures to the north and west, their reluctance to jump fences, serious predator threats to the south and parasitism to the east.

Although called a medium-sized antelope, blackbuck are relatively small as far as exotics in Texas go. Females average around 60 pounds with mature bucks reaching 80 pounds. Males often appear much larger than they are due in part to their impressive corkscrew horns that can reach lengths of more than 30 inches.

Females are tan with white underbellies while dominant males have black upper bodies instead of tan. Both sexes have white eye rings, chin patches and inner legs. Mature males are extremely black in color, thus giving the animal its moniker.

Blackbuck feed in small harem groups led by a dominant male. Males without harem groups, older rams no longer able to fight for dominance and younger bucks often travel in small bachelor groups.

Mainly grazers, blackbuck feed on a number of grasses but will occasionally browse such plants as mesquite and live oak.

With numbers in their native countries reaching all-time lows, Texas is quickly becoming one of the only places left to hunt free-ranging blackbuck.

Best Places to Hunt: As with most exotics, the highest concentrations of free-ranging blackbuck are found in the Edwards Plateau region. Blackbucks are also found in great numbers on most game ranches.

Recommended Calibers: Smaller calibers such as the .243 are more than adequate given the animal's small size.

Professional hunter Garry Wright (left) and Carlos Celaya with blackbuck antelope taken near Camp Verde.

The Extremely Exotic

Nick E. Cambell listened intently to the private's story, unsure if what he was being told could possibly be true. Cambell and a few other soldiers had been sharing stories of their youth, past girl-friends and future plans during some downtime while stationed at Fort Ord in California. But Private Reverend Royal Jacobs's story was different. It was too frightening. And too bizarre.

The story began simple enough, with Jacobs's telling of being a teenager in the small East Texas town of Longview during the mid-60s. Around 1965, he recalled, a 13-year-old boy named John-ny Maples had stirred the town's imagination and fear with a sto-ry that he had seen a 7-foot ape roaming the woods. A short time following the boy's story, two people had been found killed, their bodies literally torn to pieces. A posse was formed to hunt down a beast but all that was ever found were large foot imprints.

Although Jacobs's story sounds more like something out of a horror movie than real life in Texas, research (and several news clippings) gave the story some credibility. The only thing in doubt is whether or not the ape really existed. Today, many Texans won-der the same thing; is Texas home to some, as yet unidentified, ape-like creature?

Known in various parts of the state as Bigfoot, Sasquatch, skunk ape, bush ape or desert ape, the first recorded sighting of this type of creature in Texas was in 1837. Since then there have been thousands of sightings and currently there are more than 100 eyewitness accounts per year. No one believes in the creature's existence more than the members of the Texas Bigfoot Research Center, who as they state, "exist to validate what we believe to be an undocumented species of bipedal primate."

In 2002, TBRC formally asked TPWD to grant the creature legal protection. TPWD responded that it only has authority over known and indigenous species. Regardless of its legal status (or existence) TBRC strongly encourages hunters not to shoot Big-foot if they see one.

Fallow or European Fallow
Cervus dama

With large palmate antlers similar to those of the moose, fallow deer are one of the most impressive and sought after exotics in Texas. Originally from the Mediterranean regions of Europe and Asia, fallow are one of the most introduced animals in the world, with healthy populations found on every continent except Antarctica. As of 1988, there were an estimated 15,000 fallow in Texas alone, most of which reside in the Edwards Plateau region.

Fallow are large deer standing 38 inches at the shoulder with mature males topping the scales at more than 220 pounds. Males have impressive antlers with palmate areas as wide as 25 inches. Fallow coloration varies greatly around the world, but in Texas, black, white and tan with white spots are the most common.

Kevin "Junior" Miller with a spotted fallow taken near Harper.

Because of the wide range of fallow in Texas, food sources vary but most are predominately grazers with some browsing. Although adaptable to most environments, fallows prefer grassy areas with tree cover available for shelter.

Best Places to Hunt: Free-ranging animals are mostly concentrated in the Edwards Plateau region although healthy numbers exist in bordering regions as well. All colorations of fallow are popular on game ranches.

Recommended Calibers: Any larger deer rifle calibers such as the .270, .30-06, or 7mm are more than sufficient.

Feral Animals

By definition a feral animal is one that has "escaped domestication and become wild." Once free from human control, these animals often wreak havoc on delicate ecosystems, compete with native species, spread disease and cause untold millions of dollars in damage.

Feral animals have been a problem in Texas since the arrival of the first European explorers. Despite their best efforts to keep stock and pets contained, explorers and colonists lost countless horses, cattle, pigs, goats, dogs, cats and fowl to the call of the wild. Of these, only horses and cattle are no longer believed to be found ranging freely throughout the state. Not only did the remaining species multiply, but untold numbers join them each year through accidental escape, release or abandonment.

Today, the most numerous feral animal in Texas is easily the pig. It is estimated that there is one feral hog for every ten humans in Texas. Although wild pigs offer excellent sporting opportunities, their ever-growing numbers are becoming more and more problematic. Feral hogs destroy, eat or strip everything in their path, making them extremely unpopular to farmers, ranchers, rural landowners and even those living in the suburbs or along golf courses.

Feral goats also offer great hunting opportunities but aren't nearly as widespread as are feral pigs. They are found in pockets throughout the state but are more numerous in west and south Texas where they are sometimes referred to as Spanish goats or brush rams. Feral goats aren't nearly as destructive as wild hogs, but due to their surefooted nature and ability to maneuver through any type of terrain they often end up devastating delicate areas that take years to rebound.

Feral cats are second only to hogs in terms of ecological damage. It is estimated that the nearly 70 million feral cats in the United States kill more than a billion small mammals and hundreds of millions of birds a year. In addition, feral cats also kill small reptiles and amphibians. Their ecological impact is so great that some experts argue that feral cats are actually more detrimental to Texas than are hogs. Unfortunately, feral cats are found in every part of the state and despite various control methods in urban areas, their numbers show no sign of decreasing.

Feral dogs are an ever-growing problem in Texas. Much like cats and hogs, feral dogs are highly adaptable and are found in every part of the state. They are especially problematic in rural and poor areas. Feral dogs often run in packs, are extremely aggressive and much like cats, often kill for the thrill of killing rather than for food. In some areas, it is believed that feral dogs kill more livestock than does any other predator. Just how dangerous feral dogs can be became horrifically clear outside St. Louis, Missouri, in March 2001 when 10-year-old Rodney McAllister was mauled to death by a pack of dogs in a park near his home. With the population of feral dogs being continually increased by more and more of the so-called "dangerous" breeds of dogs, such as pit bulls, Rottweilers and Dobermans, incidents such as this may become more and more common.

Several species of feral birds have established large numbers throughout Texas. The most widespread of these is easily the pigeon. Pigeons can be found in almost every major city in Texas in huge numbers. They are also found in agricultural fields and near grain elevators. In some rural areas, pigeons are hunted for sport or shot or poisoned for control efforts.

Feral guinea fowl, peafowl (peacock), ducks and chickens have all established colonies in various parts of the state. Some of these, such as guinea fowl, peafowl and ducks offer unique hunting opportunities with the promise of a highly unusual trophy.

Although found on exotic ranches, most rheas, emus and ostriches were imported into Texas as livestock. In the early 1990s, many farmers and ranches began breeding the birds for meat, feathers, eggs and leather. By the late 1990s, it became quite apparent that the market for these products didn't exist in Texas and many birds were either slaughtered or released into the wild. Rheas and emus faired the best and can occasionally be found scattered throughout the state.

Monk parakeet

Originally imported from the lowlands of South America for the pet trade, Monk parakeets (*Myiopsitta monachus*) are found in various sized colonies in Dallas, Ft. Worth, Grand Prairie, Houston, Waxahachie and probably elsewhere. Similar in color, the red crowned parrot (*Amazona viridigenalis*) from eastern Mexico is another member of the avian pet trade to make a successful jump into the wild. It can be found in healthy numbers in several cities in the Rio Grande Valley. The beautiful coloring of these exotic birds makes them a favorite among birdwatchers and photographers who often forget just how detrimental to the ecosystem they can be.

Although not found in large numbers anywhere in the state, many non-native breeds of snakes, lizards, turtles and crocodilian have all been found roaming freely. Generally the result of escape or an unwanted pet, these reptiles pose serious threats to native species and in urban areas, to smaller dogs and cats.

Regardless of the sporting potential that these animals offer, be it hunting or photography, feral animals are a huge problem in Texas and one that's only getting worse.

Hogs
Sus scrofa

Today we camped at Tejocote Creek, having traveled 14 miles; the pigs found at this place were as big as a five or six-month-old calf.

> — José Enrique de la Peña, 1836

The wild hog also is frequently met with, and, although it has never been known to make a voluntary attack upon a man, yet, when provoked, it is a very furious and formidable animal. These hogs are descended from the domestic swine, and have become wild by running at large in the woods.

> — Mary Austin Holley, 1836

Feral hogs have been in Texas for so long and are so prolific that most people forget that they're not indigenous to the state. There are an estimated 2 million feral hogs in Texas and Texas Parks and Wildlife admits this number is probably on the low end. Hogs are second only to whitetails in terms of game hunted in the state.

In Texas, feral hogs are of a mixed, if not completely complicated, lineage. They are descendants of escaped European domesticated hogs as well as European wild hogs released for sport hunting by early settlers. With erect dorsal hair that resembles a Mohawk, sharp, protruding tusks, and an almost indestructible hide, many argue that Russian boars must be included in the mix somewhere as well. While this matter is highly contested, in Texas the term "Russian" has become a synonym for hogs with these characteristics.

Feral hogs roam throughout the state, inhabiting almost every type of topography, but seem to be most prolific in the eastern and southern portions of the state. Regardless of where they live, evidence of their existence is easy to find due to the destruction they leave in their path.

Hogs are a combination of bulldozer and garbage disposal. They will eat almost anything, including crops, browse, forbs, roots, fruit, small animals and carrion. They can destroy fields by rooting for food or by creating shallow depressions called wallows. They can eliminate such ground-nesting species as quail and turkeys from an area by destroying nests and nesting sites and can destroy fences traveling to their next destination.

Hogs in Texas vary in weight and height due to the numerous bloodlines and breeds in the mix but most stand around 40 inches and weigh between 100 to 300 pounds. Hogs of between 400 to 700 pounds are not unheard of although the latter is fairly rare.

Author Gayne C. Young with a "meat hog" taken near Crystal City.

With such large size, razor type tusks and an unstoppable tenacity, hog hunting in Texas can be an extremely exciting—or nerve racking—undertaking. Some hunters compound the rush by hunting with dogs and either handgun or knife (yes, knife). For those not looking for quite as much excitement, hunting from stands, over water holes or by spot and stalk are the most common methods.

Best Places to Hunt: Feral hogs are found almost everywhere in Texas although they tend to be rare in the western portion of the state. Hunts in the eastern portion of the state as well as in the South Texas Plains region are extremely popular and can produce good trophies.

Recommended Calibers: Although hogs are shot with almost everything from .30-30s to .45-70s, larger calibers with "knock down" power are highly recommended. Hunters opting to take hogs with a handgun would do best with .357, .44 or the newer Smith & Wesson .500. Slug guns or shotguns with buckshot are good choices in thicker cover.

Creating a Better Boar

Walt Wendler with a big Barr hog taken in Brazos Valley

Some landowners in search of larger boars for themselves or their clients to hunt have turned to an old farming technique: castration. As with domestic animals, the result has been impressive. Once trapped in heavy steel traps, the chosen males are castrated before being released back into the wild. After castration, these barrow hogs, or Barr hogs, often balloon in bulk (some weigh more than 400 pounds) and ferocious disposition.

The resulting animals have produced such good trophies that some scoring organizations, such as Weiser Weight and Tusk, have developed a Barr category for both free-range and estate hogs.

Nilgai
Boselaphus tragocamelus

An extremely large antelope native to India and Pakistan, Nilgai can measure up to 5 feet at the shoulder and weigh close to 700 pounds. Males have small, bi-curved horns that average only 7 inches in height

Author Gayne C. Young with a mature bull nilgai
taken near Raymondville with outfitter Garry Wright.

with 11 inches being a terrific trophy. Males also sport beards of hair from their lower neck that can reach in excess of 5 inches in length.

Nilgai are tan to brown or gray to dark gray with mature males taking on a bluish sheen. Because of this, nilgai are also referred to as blue bulls or blue bucks. Both sexes have thick skin with males having even thicker skin covering their chest and neck. This undoubtedly offers great protection from the numerous thorn and barb-bearing vegetation of the South Texas Plains and Gulf Prairies and Marshes regions they inhabit.

Nilgai are fairly diurnal, being active mostly in the early morning and evening hours. During the breeding season males gather harem groups and become extremely territorial. They mark their territory with large dung piles that they are constantly adding to. If threatened or challenged, however, males will fight by utilizing their thick neck muscles to "neck wrestle" or by using their small horns to spar.

Due to their large size, nilgai have few predators in their native Asia. Only tigers and man are of any serious threat to adults. In Texas, nilgai have even fewer predators although calves are susceptible to coyotes and other large predatory and opportunistic animals.

Nilgai have eyesight and hearing equal to, if not better than, whitetails. Their sense of smell is considered to be poor at best.

Best Places to Hunt: Free-ranging nilgai are found in the Gulf Prairies and Marshes and South Texas Plains regions.

Recommended Calibers: Given their immense size and forward thick hides anything less than .375 H & H or .416 isn't recommended. Nilgai are big game animals in the same vein as their African cousins.

Sika
Cervus nippon

Just as with feral hogs, sika deer in Texas are from a mixed lineage. Since the 1930s three varieties of sika deer—Japanese, Formosan and Dybowski—have been introduced to Texas. All three varieties are from Asia. Hybridization of the three occurred as the deer spread throughout the Edwards Plateau and South Texas plains region. Because of this, weight, height and color vary greatly.

Sika deer in Texas range in weight from anywhere between 100 and 240 pounds. In height, they vary between 30 and 43 inches tall at the shoulder. Coloration can be brown to extremely dark brown with some animals having faint spots. Males sport antlers with 3 to 4 points per beam. Each beam can obtain a height of more than 30 inches, although 14 inches tends to be the average.

In their native Asia, sika deer are rapidly losing territory and in some parts of the continent are becoming extremely rare. In Texas,

Author Gayne C. Young with sika deer taken near Kerrville.

with no natural predators except man, their numbers continue to increase. Their current population is estimated in the tens of thousands.

Best Places to Hunt: Free-range sika can be found throughout the Edwards Plateau and South Texas Plains regions of the state. Sikas are also popular on most game ranches.

Recommended Calibers: Larger deer rifle calibers such as .270 and above are adequate.

Texas Snow Monkeys

What started out as an act of kindness quickly turned into an ever-multiplying barrel of trouble for ranchers in and around the small town of Dilley, Texas, south of San Antonio.

Hearing that a troop of 150 Japanese snow monkeys near Kyoto, Japan, had worn out their welcome, Lou Griffin and her husband had the simians moved to a small compound on their ranch in Dilley. By 1995, the troop had swelled to more than 600 animals. When Griffin later filed for divorce, ownership of the ranch became a court matter, during which time the compound fell into disarray. Sensing that the electric fence no longer worked, several of the red-faced, 2-foot tall macaques ventured onto the surrounding mesquite covered flats in search of food. Although most of the simians have since been recovered, monkey sightings are far from rare.

Having seen the wayward monkeys more than once, hunting guide Joey Burleson of Pearsall comments, "Yeah, it's kind of weird to be driving around a ranch and see a monkey off in the distance, sitting on a fence post."

HISTORIC BIG GAME

Because of sound conservation and a few progressive thinking individuals and organizations, most of the original big game of Texas still roam the state. Only two species, bison and elk, are no longer listed as game animals. But this doesn't mean that these two have vanished from the state altogether. Quite the contrary is true.

Although listed as an exotic by Texas Parks and Wildlife, thousands of bison and elk remain in Texas on private game ranches and some larger cattle ranches.

Bison
Bos bison

You would scarcely believe me, were I to tell you of the vast herds of buffalo which abound here; I have frequently seen a thousand in a day between this place, and the mouth of Little River.
— W. B. Dewees, 1822

One must ...be on one's guard against the fury of these buffalo. When one has been wounded, it chased the hunters, even lying in wait with determination at the foot of the trees that they were obliged to climb and trying to uproot them with their feet until they had received the fatal shot.
— The Talon brothers, 1698

...it is timid until wounded, but then its impetuosity is irresistible, and its attacks are repeated until it falls...Should it discover and throw down its antagonist, it gores and tramples upon him until it falls dead by his side.
— Gen. Arthur Goodall Wavel, 1835

The plight of the bison, or American buffalo, is well known to anyone who ever paid attention in history class. In order to serve the fur trade and to aid in the extermination of the American Indian, bison were slaughtered by the millions. Were it not for a few forward thinking individuals, what has become for many a symbol of the American West would have gone the way of the dinosaur.

Despite the fact that they once roamed the western two-thirds of the state in the tens of millions, bison are considered an exotic species and are confined to a few cattle ranches, parks and game ranches.

Standing more than 5 feet at the shoulder and weighing between 1,500 and 2,000 pounds, bison are truly behemoths. They are brownish black with thick, shaggy fur covering their head, neck, shoulders and forelegs. Horns are black, short and curve upward.

Bison are mainly grazers although some forbs are digested. They live and travel in large herds with the exception of older, solitary males. These males, just as are older bovine bulls, can be aggressive and testy if approached.

Bison are diurnal and spend most of their day grazing. In an effort to keep cool or remove bothersome insects, bison will wallow, sometimes creating large, shallow sores within the ground.

Best Places to Hunt: Bison are available on some game ranches.

Recommended Calibers: Bison are large animals with thick skin and a nasty temperament when injured. Many hunters choosing to take bison today opt to make it a "historic" hunt and select their weapons accordingly, often taking to the field with big bored buffalo rifles in .45-70, .40-90, .45-110, or .50-90 calibers. Most modern calibers intended for African game such as the .375 H & H or .416 are also good choices.

An English Buffalo Safari

After much consideration and having acquired men and supplies, Jerry B. St. John, Esq. of Great Britain decided to allow himself six weeks for safari. The vast wilderness along the Gulf Coast of the recently formed Republic of Texas looked more than promising. Judging by the stories he'd heard around the docks where his ship was being repaired, the interior was bounding with game. If the estimates of the Caddo Indian guides he'd hired were correct, six weeks would provide excellent hunting and be more than enough time to take a trophy buffalo.

In the early summer of 1842, St. John and his party began their journey inward from the southern coastline, near the modern-day cities of Beaumont and Port Arthur. St. John's party consisted of roughly 20 men, "...six of whom were white men, the rest Caddo Indians." Despite the heat and relatively difficult travel, the party made good time and by the second day of May they had established camp at the edge of an island of timber nestled between Pedro Bayou and Burnet Creek.

The hunting camp was without the modern comfort of tents, but all men in the party slept and relaxed within the confines of huts erected with "poles and boughs" by some of the Caddos in the party. These accommodations were more than "luxurious" and St. John found that they helped add a certain roughness to the camp that made the safari much more enjoyable.

Meals were taken at the front of the camp, next to the fire where party members could eat and peer outwards onto the "boundless interminable prairie" that lay before them. With very little in the way of "corn, meal and potatoes," meals consisted of little more than meat. Grey squirrel, wild turkey and plenty of venison were served at almost every sitting. At first, St. John and his European counterparts were concerned at their new diet of mostly meat, but soon realized that "...living in the open air, in the constant pursuit of game, riding and walking vast and incredible distances in an exceedingly short space of time, are much greater incentives to digestion than a lazy stroll through St. James's Park."

Members of the hunting party needed all the protein they could get as the day-to-day rigors of hunting were more than taxing. Days were spent riding long distances across the Gulf Coastal Prairie, along rivers and through islands of timber with thick underbrush in search of game. Game was so abundant St. John later wrote of his trip that "...each day [was] fresh and varied—each day presenting some new feature—now a deer, then a hog; now geese and swans, then a conager; now a possum, then a coon." But despite an abundance and variety of game, the party had yet to find any buffalo, the species St. John wanted most of all. His hopes were answered only a few days into the hunt by the sound of thunder.

The men had just finished breakfast when the rolling bass sounds of thunder filled the air. With the sky deep blue and free from clouds, members of the hunting party looked to the distance, trying to locate the coming storm. Instead of dark clouds they spotted a prairie exploding in dust and debris.

"What is this?" St. John yelled, questioning anyone within the party who might know.

One of the Caddo Indians responded, "Buffalo."

The immense dust storm and the bison that led it raced closer and closer to camp with a force that shook the ground and everything that stood upon it. The herd was estimated to be 400 to 500 in number, advancing at a hurried speed across the prairie. The men quickly ran to a nearby thicket to seek safety behind the trees. From there they would shoot at the passing herd and give chase to those that didn't fall.

As the herd dissected the prairie before him, St. John voiced his thankfulness of the hunting party's choice in tactics. "The herd came near the grove; and it was fortunate we were closely sheltered. For instant death from feet and horns would have been our fate, had we been in the open savannah," he wrote.

The men waited at the edge of the thicket as each minute the herd drew closer and closer to within shooting range. As it approached, St. John picked out his first trophy.

"At the head of the herd was a huge, black bull who was their leader, guiding them in their onward course; he came along, bellowing like a hundred lions, his tail straight on end, like a mopstick, and at times tossing up the earth with powerful horns."

St. John and others in his immediate surroundings took aim and fired. They fired, reloaded and fired again until the gigantic black bull and several others fell to the earth. The herd, unable to stop, galloped over their former leader and continued along the unseen trail. St. John ran out to inspect his first trophy, but gave himself little time to admire it. He quickly instructed two Indians to begin butchering the animals while he and the rest of the hunters followed the herd.

The hunting party caught up with the still thundering herd in less than an hour. At the sight of the men, three buffalo split from the herd. This group split once more as a large bull abruptly veered away from the other two. To better follow the herd, the hunters would have to split as well. With a few men riding beside him, St. John spurred after the bull as the remainder of the hunting party continued chasing the larger herd.

Still mounted, St. John and an Indian companion dropped the huge bull in its tracks after a short chase. Although down, the bull still required a pistol shot to the head from St. John to finish him off. The men began butchering the animal, with great haste so they could catch up to the party and perhaps join in taking more bison.

After completing a hasty field dressing, St. John and his companions took up the trail of the herd and the rest of the hunting party. They were traveling parallel to a creek that was skirted on both sides by small bands of timber when the air was suddenly shattered with the sharp crack of gunfire. At first, St. John attributed the shots to his fellow hunter's success but quickly realized that their success could mean his death.

The distant hunting party's shots had inadvertently turned the herd toward St. John. "Our position was far from being an agreeable one: to stand still was death, to take to our heels across the prairie was to risk being overtaken by angry beasts. The Indian decided the question by dismounting and taking to the cover of the nearest thicket. I followed his example as quickly as possible; and having secured our horses, we grasped our rifles and prepared for action."

The thundering herd ripped across the plains less than 50 yards from where St. John and his companions took refuge. From the safety of the trees, St. John singled out a fat cow and dropped it with one shot to the beast's head. No sooner had the cow dropped than the rest of the hunting party screamed by the thicket in pursuit. St. John left the cow to be butchered later and spurred after the fleeing hunters. By the time he reached the men they had dropped seven more bulls and were stopping to inspect their trophies.

Lt. Snow was about to dismount when one of the "dead" bulls suddenly rose from the prairie floor and charged. He jerked the reins to turn, but the horse's response came too late. In a blur of motion, the bull collided into the side of the horse. The sound of pounding flesh was echoed by the shrill cries of the horse as one of the bull's horns pierced its side. Snow hit the ground with the force of a comet. Gasping for air, he turned to see the bull shaking the horse's dead body like a rag doll in an effort to free itself.

Snow lunged for his rifle and fired a half dozen times into the trapped bull. At the last shot, the bull staggered and fell, collapsing in a heap to the side of the horse it was still attached to by its horn.

That evening members of the hunting party lazed around the fire drinking coffee, eating bison, smoking and telling stories of the day's events.

"It is my firm conviction that, by our twenty men, no less a quantity than a hundred weight of buffalo was devoured," St. John wrote. "Ribs, steaks, hearts, livers, brains, went the way of all flesh, with a rapidity and dexterity most remarkable."

Later, when all were gorged on meat and good times, St. John retired for the evening, noting "There was not one who did not woo slumber as the best and most true refreshment after our day's labour."

—*Portions of this piece first appeared in* True West Magazine

Elk or Wapiti
Cervus elaphus

...the woods and prairies about us not only afforded excellent grazing for our cattle and horses, but teemed with every species of game—elk, deer, bears, wild turkeys, and, at the proper season, buffalo and mustang.

— George Kendall, 1814

This lake is surrounded by the best stock-raising country in the world, and the wild cattle, horses, deer and elk resort to it in the thousands.

— George W. Bonnell, 1840

Just as with big horn sheep, whether or not today's wapiti or elk are true native Texas species is a matter of personal interpretation and definition. The elk seen by early Anglo explorers and settlers was *Cervus merriami*, a species that became extinct around 1900. In 1928, Judge J.C. Hunter released 44 *Cervus elaphus* imported from North Dakota into the Guadalupe Mountains in an attempt to reintroduce elk. Ten years later the herd had expanded to 400 animals. Today's free-ranging elk are descendants of Hunter's herd and any new stock that private landowners in the western portion of the state have released. To some, these deer should be considered a native species. To others, they are an exotic.

Even Texas Parks and Wildlife has a hard time deciding how to classify elk. Once listed as a game animal, elk have only recently been awarded exotic status.

Best Places to Hunt: With most free-ranging elk herds existing on private land, most hunts are arranged through landowners or an outfitter. Elk are extremely popular on game ranches throughout the state.

Recommended Calibers: Due to an elk's large size, .300 Winchester Mag., .300 WSM, .300 Weatherby or higher are recommended.

3

PREDATORY GAME

Alligators, mountain lions, bobcats and the rest of the animals in this chapter are difficult to place into a specific category. Although legally hunted, most hunters do not consider them to be game animals. Despite the fact that they are all carnivores and posses the ability to turn on their pursuer, they are not considered to be dangerous game. Some of these animals are trapped for their fur, but not all are furbearing and of the ones that are, only foxes make the state's fur-bearing category.

Hunters who specialize in "calling" claim that coyotes, bobcats and foxes are predatory animals but then this same group often categorizes animals such as the smaller and far less dangerous raccoons and ringtails as predators as well. Even Texas Parks and Wildlife seems hard pressed to correctly categorize this group of animals. Under legal definitions, alligators, mountain lions and bobcats are labeled as "non-game" animals, a group that also includes porcupines, turtles, some squirrels, rabbits and armadillos. To most hunters, the idea of placing the alligator, one of the largest carnivores on the planet, in the same group as fuzzy bunnies seems completely off kilter.

Regardless of where these animals truly fit in categorically, all offer a potentially thrilling hunt with the slightest possibility that, due to their predatory nature, things could turn intense. For that reason, this chapter is entitled Predatory Game.

Alligator
Alligator mississippiensis

With tremendous strength, a muscular tail capable of breaking bone with a single blow and jaws able to generate 2,000 pounds of pressure, the American alligator is undoubtedly one of the state's most formidable yet overlooked big game animals.

Once teetering on the brink of extinction, the American alligator has made a tremendous comeback since being listed as endangered in Texas in 1973. Today, the species is listed as a protected game animal and special permits are required to hunt them. Most alligator hunting takes place on state wildlife management areas, but landowners with healthy numbers of alligators on their property are also issued permits that they in turn sell to hunters.

Alligators are the largest reptiles in North America. They are capable of reaching 20-plus feet in length, although in Texas they rarely exceed 14. Larger males can weigh in excess of 600 pounds. Hatchlings are black with yellowish cross band stripes while adults are extremely dark black with a yellowish to white belly.

As the top predator in the areas it inhabits, alligators will eat anything they can catch, including fish, turtles, small mammals, birds, snakes and other alligators. Larger alligators also feed on deer and boar. Despite their ferocious appearance, alligators pose very little threat to humans so long as they are unprovoked. However, small children and pets should be kept at a safe distance from the water when in gator country.

First-time alligator hunter Hillary Henderson with her trophy, an 11-foot-plus gator taken at Mad Island WMA.

Best Places to Hunt: Alligators are scattered throughout the Pineywoods and Gulf Prairies and Marshes regions. The state issues hunting permits to landowners with alligators who in turn sell them to outfitters or hunters directly. Several state wildlife management areas offer alligator hunts through state drawings. **NOTE:** Hunters wishing to sell the hides must purchase a separate CITES (Convention on International Trade of Endangered Species) tag from the state.

Recommended Calibers: Most alligators are dispatched after they have been hooked, snared or shot with an arrow with a line attached. For this reason shots at close range are the norm. Shotgun slugs or larger handgun calibers are most often used. Buckshot is not recommended.

The Game's Afoot

While most hunters are familiar with displaying trophies in a place of prominence on a wall, few hunters consider, or are even aware of, the possibilities of wearing their trophies on their feet. Most trophy animals can be processed into exceptional leather that can in turn be crafted into exquisite and unique belts, slings, wallets and boots.

But not all skins are suited to footwear. As Richard Sanders of *Russell Moccasins* explains, "Deerskin, elk and moose, while very nice leathers, tend to be too soft and stretchy for boots. Softer leathers like these can be used as trim or accents. But animals such as water buffalo, alligator, eland and nilgai game make great boots."

A pair of beautiful custom made wallets from Walden & Bork.

Not only do these leathers make great boots, but the cost is generally the same as with custom-made cow leather boots. Those not wishing to put their game afoot have plenty of other options. Companies such as *Walden & Bork* can turn almost any game skin into any number of items, including personal accessories, wallets, handbags, notebook covers, cigar cases, place mats, tote bags and luggage.

By turning game skins into leather, hunters have more than one way to remember the hunt.

Bobcat
Lynx rufus

The bobcat has become the most prolific cat in the state due in part to its adaptability. Although it prefers rocky canyons and outcrops, bobcats can be found in almost every part of the state. Even the famous naturalist John James Audubon commented on how surprised he was to find the animal living upon the open and unprotected plains. As human encroachment continues, the bobcat is quickly discovering that it can live just as easily in the rough areas surrounding golf courses and suburbs as it can in the wild.

Bobcats are considered a medium-sized cat weighing in average between 11 and 35 pounds and obtaining nearly 3 feet in length. They are reddish-brown with black spots covering their upper body and legs. Their lower legs and the rim of their ears are striped black while their underbellies are white. Their short, "bobbed" tail gives the animal its moniker.

Perhaps one of the keys to the bobcat's successful spread into human habitat is its diet. Bobcats tend to prefer the smaller animals that coexist or benefit from living within close confines of humans. Generally, the bulk of the bobcat's diet consists of smaller rodents, rabbits, squirrels, and birds. Larger game such as deer and turkeys are also utilized. An opportunistic eater, bobcats will eat carrion in addition to preying on smaller domesticated animals such as sheep, goats and fowl.

Male bobcats mark their territory and travel routes by dropping feces on large rocks and other raised objects as well as by making what are called scrapes by urinating on piles of leaves, twigs and other plant material.

Like all cats, the bobcat has exceptional vision, especially at night. Because of this and their generally shy and retreating nature, bobcats are mostly nocturnal although some may venture out before sundown or well after sunrise. It is during these brief daylight hours that most bobcats are opportunistically taken by hunters in pursuit of other game. Hunters who actively seek bobcat generally hunt either by calling or with dogs.

Bobcats are classified as furbearers in Texas. A CITES tag (available from Texas Parks and Wildlife) is required to transport the trophy animal out of state or to sell.

Best Places to Hunt: Bobcats are found throughout the state.

Recommended Calibers: Smaller calibers such as .22 Mag., .22 Hornet, .222, .223, or .243 are more than adequate. A 12-gauge shotgun #4 pellet is also a good choice.

Call Them In

Coyotes, bobcats, cougars, foxes, raccoons and a host of other predatory animals and even some game animals can be lured into shooting range by emulating various animal sounds. The best of these "calls" are those of animals in distress, mating animals or animal vocalizations. By tricking an animal that it is coming after a younger animal in distress or the sound of a free meal, an experienced "caller" can bring an animal to within yards of where he's hidden. Calling is exciting, addictive and relatively easy to learn.

Perhaps the best way to begin calling is by utilizing one of the many electronic callers on the market today. *Burnham Brothers, Johnny Stewart, Hunters Specialties, Foxpro,* and *Primos* all make calling devices that utilize prerecorded sounds from a CD or Digital Memory Card. These units are small, compact and relatively inexpensive.

More experienced callers often utilize specially designed mouth-blown calls. Made of wood or plastic, these mouth calls can be divided into three categories: closed reed, open reed and howlers. While these type of calling devices are considerably more affordable than electronic calling devices, they are far more difficult to master.

Inexperienced callers might consider booking a hunt with an outfitter that specializes in calling animals or research the methods through print magazines or in books such as *Successful Predator Hunting* by Michael Schoby. Regardless of how you practice the art of calling, the result is often exciting.

Coyote
Canis latrans

For an animal that has not only survived decades of eradication programs initiated and regulated by ranchers, as well as state and federal governments, and successfully adapted to almost every environment in the state, the coyote gets little respect. Most individuals see the coyote as a worthless scavenger or as a lazy, opportunistic livestock killer. Even the coyote's nicknames of little wolf, prairie wolf and brush wolf refer to the coyote's similarities to another animal rather than to the coyote itself. Public relation issues aside, the coyote is a highly cunning and successful predatory animal.

The coyote is a medium size dog-like carnivore that ranges between 30 to 45 pounds and averages 48 inches in length. It is grayish brown to black on top with a yellowish underbelly. Its bushy tail is black tipped. Coyote fur is especially prized and ranks only behind the raccoon in terms of Texas sales to fur markets.

Although similar in appearance to Gray wolves, the coyote is much smaller and much more successful, having survived and flourished in spite of the eradication programs that targeted both animals. Coyotes thrive where wolves once lived.

Living up to their reputation as opportunists, coyotes will eat anything they can get their jaws around, from refuse to livestock. They eat carrion, fruit, small game, such as rabbits and squirrels, deer and antelope fawns, snakes, frogs and chickens. If it can be digested, chances are that the coyote will attempt to eat it. They are the buzzards of the ground.

Coyotes can be active anytime of the day or night but tend to be more so late in the evening and early in the morning. They congregate in family groups, packs or travel alone.

As an animal that relies much on vocal communication and its sensitive hearing to find prey, coyotes are traditionally hunted by calling. Hunters imitate or play recorded sounds of wounded animals or social calls to lure coyotes into shooting range. When done at night with a red colored lens covering the light source, coyote calling, like all predator calling, can be a real adrenaline rush with coyotes charging toward the caller with breakneck speed.

Best Places to Hunt: Coyotes are found throughout the state.

Recommended Calibers: Although coyotes are shot with anything and everything, smaller calibers such as .222, .223 and .243 are more than adequate.

Choosing a Taxidermist

Trophies are by far the best reminder of a time enjoyed afield. But unfortunately these visual reminders are often compromised in quality because of poor taxidermy workmanship.

"Too often hunters don't think about a taxidermist until the hunt is over," says Rhodes Taxidermy owner Gary Broach. "But the best time to think about a taxidermist is long before you even take to the field."

By consulting a taxidermist beforehand, hunters stand a better chance of receiving the mount of their dreams. Not only can a taxidermist assist hunters by arranging shipment of their trophy from field to home, but often times he or she can offer advice on where some of the best game is coming from, what clients are saying about their outfitters and the best methods of field preparation.

Additionally, a taxidermist can provide a wealth of information on what he or she needs to ensure the most realistic looking mount.

"Some animals need to be measured before they're skinned, some don't," says Broach. "Some need to be measured in a specific way. For example, the measurements taken on cats aren't anywhere near the same as are those needed for, say, a nilgai bull."

Of course, all the knowledge of what to do in the field and how to ship trophies doesn't insure a quality mount. For that, hunters need to do their homework and ask plenty of questions.

Things to consider when choosing a taxidermist:

Years of experience: There's nothing wrong with giving business to an up-and-coming taxidermist. However, what the taxidermist did before opening shop can make a world of difference. Don't be afraid to ask what type of training the taxidermist had prior to hanging out a shingle. Did he or she intern with another taxidermist? Do they have references? Are there examples of the type of work you can expect?

Physical shop: By its very definition, taxidermy isn't the cleanest of professions. Mounting an animal takes a lot of supplies and produces a lot of mess but that shouldn't carry over into the showroom or office. Professional taxidermists are just that: professionals. The area that customers see should reflect that.

Customer referrals: By some estimates up to 80 percent of a taxidermist's business is from returning customers. People generally don't go back to a business that offers mediocre service or poor workmanship. Ask for a list of referrals when seeking a taxidermist. Friends and fellow hunters are also a good source for taxidermy recommendations. The next time you compliment a mount ask who did it.

Ask questions, make your requests known: Don't be afraid to ask questions about your mount, costs involved or turn-around time. If you don't like the answers you get, tell the taxidermist what you expect or go somewhere else. Most taxidermists, like most business persons, will go out of his or her way to accommodate a customer. A good taxidermist knows that a happy customer is not only a return customer but is also likely to recommend his or her services to others.

Cost: The saying, "You get what you pay for" has never applied more than in the world of taxidermy. Some taxidermists cut corners by using less than stellar supplies or by not giving the project enough time. As Broach explains, "There's a big difference between a $400 dollar shoulder mount and an $800 one."

FOXES

The foxhunter could find constant employment in this country.
— Mary Austin Holley, 1836

Much confusion surrounds the foxes of the Lone Star State. The first conflict comes from how many species actually reside within the state: three or four?

This dilemma arises when considering the swift and/or kit foxes that, until recently, were listed as two separate species, *Vulpes velox* and *Vulpes macrotis* respectively. Recent in-depth studies now place the swift and kit into the same species: *Vulpes velox.* Despite this scientific revelation, some people still contest that the animals are two separate creatures, regardless of the fact that no one can tell them apart.

Common gray fox

Common Gray Fox
Urocyon cinereoargenteus

Roughly the same size as the red fox, the common gray fox (pictured) is found in wooded or areas with heavy cover throughout the state. As its name implies, the gray fox is grayish with brownish to red legs. Its belly and lower neck are white. The gray fox's diet is similar to the other foxes of the state.

Gray foxes are active during both the day and night. Gray foxes are well adapted to climbing trees and often do so to escape danger, an ability that comes as a surprise to many hunters.

Recommended Calibers: Nothing larger than .223 is recommended.

Red Fox
Vulpes vulpes

Of European origin, the red fox was first released into the wild in 1895. It has the distinction of being one of the few, if not the only, predatory animals deliberately released into the state for the purposes of sport hunting. After its initial release, the red fox quickly spread across the state. Although rare in some areas, today the red fox can be found in almost every vegetational region of the state.

True to their name, red foxes are reddish with black tipped ears and black-banded legs. The animal's underbelly is white. Red foxes are slightly larger than the swift fox, averaging between 7 and 11 pounds. Much like the swift fox, red foxes eat a variety of smaller mammals, birds, lizards, insects and anything else they can catch or find. Unlike the swift fox, however, the red fox tends to be more active during daylight hours.

Swift or Kit Fox
Vulpes velox

The swift (or kit) fox is a small animal, not much larger than a house cat, averaging between 3 and 7 pounds. They inhabit the open desert or grasslands of the western third of the state. Their diet consists of small mammals such as rodents, jackrabbits and cottontails, lizards, insects, fish and birds. They are brownish yellow with a long, grayish-black tail.

Naturally curious, swift foxes are easily trapped or taken by opportunistic hunters in pursuit of other game.

Mountain Lion
Felis concolor

I saw game in large numbers; a panther as large as a small cow.
— Viktor Bracht, 1847

It had a large round head, with large dangerous looking tusks, was six feet long exclusive of the tail, which was two and a half feet in length. The color was that of a deer in the summer; its weight full 300, and it measured when killed 15 inches around the arm.
— Description of mountain lion taken near Bonham in 1853

When pursued by a pack, he runs well for a little distance, but soon tires, and will then take to a tree, selecting one that leans well to one side, for he is not a good climber. Out of reach of the dogs he stands upright on a horizontal branch, and calmly surveys his vociferous and baffled pursuers. Should a man appear on the scene, he ceases to watch the dogs, and dropping into a crouching position on the branch, prepares for a spring. Under such circumstances I would advise no one to approach within thirty or even forty feet. He is now, of course, easily bagged, but no bungler with the rifle should be allowed to shoot at him, as, when wounded, he is a desperate and most formidable antagonist.

— Col. Richard Irving Dodge, 1877

Except for the jaguar, the mountain lion is the largest cat in the Americas with males reaching almost 200 pounds and measuring upwards of eight feet. They are tawny brown with black markings at tail's end and around the muzzle. The animal's long claws are perfectly adapted for grasping and holding prey as well as for climbing trees.

Known as cougar, puma, deer tiger, Mexican lion, catamount and panther, the mountain lion is a solitary and secretive animal. It is mostly nocturnal but occasionally ventures out before sunset and after sunrise. It beds under small, rocky overhangs, in abandoned and enlarged burrows, spaces between large rocks and in shallow impressions under tree roots or other foliage. Similar to bobcats, male mountain lions mark their territory with piles of urine-soaked leaves called scrapes.

A mountain lion, although most fond of deer, will eat almost any animal, including big horn sheep, squirrels, rabbits, foxes, coyotes, skunks and beavers. Mountain lions are also one of the few animals that seem to have little trouble in digesting porcupines. In areas with livestock, mountain lions will take horses, sheep and cows.

Mountain lions are found throughout the state. As is the case in other states, lions have little trouble in adapting to man's encroachment, finding suitable living spaces in areas near suburbs where ample food, often in the form of pets, is available.

Like other predatory game, most mountain lions are killed by opportunistic hunters in pursuit of other game. While some hunters have had success with calling, most lions are taken with the aid of dogs.

Best Places to Hunt: Although found wherever deer are, most mountain lion hunts take place in the Trans-Pecos Mountains and Basins region.

Recommended Calibers: As most hunts for mountain lion utilize dogs, shots are generally taken at fairly short distances. Because of this, .270 and .30-30 are recommended. Handgun hunters generally opt for the .357 or .44.

Bruce (left) and Lee Duncan with a pair of lions
taken in the Big Bend area in February 1950.

HISTORIC PREDATORY GAME

Unlike the historic big game of Texas, it is highly unlikely that any of the state's historic predators will ever again be legally hunted in Texas. Some, such as the grizzly bear, have been completely eradicated. Others, such as the black bear and the ocelot, only remain in extremely small and much protected numbers. Unfortunately, with regards to the historic predators of Texas, only memories remain.

BEARS

> *The whole peninsula from the Rio Sabina to San Bernardo*
> *[Matagorda Bay] abounds in deer and bear.*
> — Don José de Evis, 1785

> *There was still, at a spot near Currie's creek, a man who made*
> *his livelihood by hunting. He kept a pack of trained hounds and*
> *had killed 60 bears in the course of two years.*
> — F. L. Olmstead, 1854

Black Bear
Ursus americanus

The black bear is slowly making its way back into what is left of its home range in the Pineywoods and Trans-Pecos Mountains and Basins regions of the state. In 2000, there were at least 30 black bears in Big Bend National Park alone.

Due to its shy ways and desire to avoid human interaction, the chances of seeing a black bear while hunting are extremely rare. Still, hunters camping in areas where bear sightings have occurred should take all precautionary measures. It is illegal to harm or kill black bears in Texas.

Grizzly or Brown Bear
Ursus arctos

According to historical records, only two grizzlies, or brown bears, have ever been taken and or discovered in Texas. The most famous of these was a 1,110-pound, silver haired behemoth taken in the Davis

Mountains in 1890 by C. O. Finley and John Z. Means. The other was identified by skull remains found on the banks of the Red River in 1950. Regardless of how many grizzlies used to call Texas home, there is little doubt that the grizzly won't be returning to the state anytime soon.

The Last Grizzly

Rearing tight on the reins, C. O. Finley and John Means brought their horses to an abrupt halt within a storm of dust and frothing sweat. Below them, the thin mountain air reverberated with the howls and yelps of pack dogs attempting to bay a bear. Stumbling down a rocky bluff toward the commotion, Finley and Means paused momentarily to acknowledge the stark change in the dog's tone. Yelps of excitement changed to that of fear and the mountainside was soon littered with dozens of dogs fleeing uphill and away from danger. Confused and angered by the pack's sudden change in direction, the men hastily turned the dogs back to the carpet of thick scrub brush and the rest of the pack below them. The dogs began their descent just as the sound of a dog being mortally wounded sliced through the mountains. The men continued pushing the frightened dogs downward all the while wondering what could make almost 50 trained bear dogs flee in terror.

Finley and Means had been hunting black bear in the Davis Mountains of far West Texas for years. The bear hunts had become an annual event that friends and families looked forward to all year. The hunts were family oriented and included men, women and children, old and young alike. Liquor was prohibited during the hunt and a minister was brought along, according to Finely, to keep camp "as clean and free of bad language as possible." The hunt that began on October 29, 1890, was no exception as friends and relatives ventured from as far away as Ft. Worth and San Antonio to participate. The eventual outcome of the hunt, however, was unlike anything the party had ever experienced before.

In the first four days of the hunt, Finley, Means and the rest of the hunters had faired well, having taken "… a bear or two and some black tail deer each day." Five days later, on November 2, things changed dramatically.

Following a morning of poor luck and false leads, the dogs finally hit upon a fresh trail shortly after lunch. The mounted hunting party followed the best they could but trailing the dogs through dense thickets of shin oaks and pine proved to be almost impossible. In attempts to follow the pack from above, Finley and Means took to higher ground. After skirting the thicket for about a mile, the men crossed paths with the pack just as they entered a small clearing.

The dogs quickly bounded upon the remains of a dead, 4-year-old cow. Studying the animal, Finley and Means determined the animal had been dragged more than a hundred yards from where it had been killed. As the pack circled the area trying to reestablish the scent, the men wondered aloud at how large a bear could kill and drag a cow of that size that great a distance.

The men's discussion was cut short when the pack exploded across the clearing and onto a rock strewn cliff side. Finley and Means spurred their mounts forward in an effort to keep up. Taking the lead, Means quickly spotted the bear just ahead of the pack and shouted, "Otie, I see the old devil!"

Steering their horses at an upward angle, the men dug in their spurs trying to get parallel to the pack. The bear headed in the opposite direction, taking the pack farther downhill and into a thicket below. Finley and Means gave chase, arriving at the thicket just as the bear and the commotion that followed exited the other side. From their vantage point, all they could see was a blur of heat-distorted motion rushing across the canyon floor before vanishing into yet another stand of scrub brush.

Finley and Means cut across a rocky bluff to within 125 yards of the thicket and quickly dismounted. Saddle guns in hand, they stumbled over rocks toward the violent exchange below. Forty to 50 dogs suddenly howled toward them in a frenzy of fear and panic. Kicking and screaming, the men pushed the dogs downward and ahead of them. A cacophony of screams and yelps weighted the air, interrupted momentarily by the sound of bones snapping and the piercing sound of life being crushed from a dog.

The men continued downward until a narrow trail of visibility through the tangled vegetation allowed them their first glimpse at what the dogs so feared. Before them was a tumultuous scene of a life and death struggle. Experienced bear dogs either skirted the bear in fear or were thrown aside like limp rags. Those dogs that braved closer met slashing claws and a muzzle full of menacing teeth. Seeing their hounds being decimated, the men steadied themselves behind a rock and began firing. Each shot seemed only to further infuriate the monstrous bear that began "... to pitch and bellow like a wild bull."

Finley and Means watched in horror as one of their blue-speckled hounds yelped in pain as the bear crushed its neck and jaw and flung it aside before lashing onto another. The men continued firing, hitting the bear untold times, until the bear collapsed onto its stomach and ceased moving. The two men edged closer and closer towards the bear, guns cocked and ready to fire, until they were in 100 or so feet of the bear.

"Otie, hadn't I better put one in his old head? He looks awfully big." Means asked.

"No, let's not tear his head up, as some of us might want to keep it," Finley replied.

With some of the dogs continuing to pull at the bear with no response, the men knew the bear was dead and moved in for a closer look. It was then that Means first realized the enormity of the bear. Studying the animal's size, the gray-tipped hairs on its back and the large hump on its shoulders, Means quickly concluded what he and Finley had done.

"Otie, we have got a grizzly!" Means screamed, throwing his hat up in the air.

Shortly thereafter, the rest of the hunting party finally arrived. Seeing the 1,100-pound behemoth that Finley and Means had taken, the hunting party couldn't help but cheer and give shouts of praise. In the decades to come, the Finley-Means grizzly would be accepted as the last grizzly taken in Texas.

— *Portions of this piece first appeared in* True West Magazine

BIG CATS

Texas once had the distinction of being home to six species of cats: jaguar, mountain lion, bobcat, ocelot, margay and jaguarondi. Of these, only the mountain lion, bobcat, jaguarondi and ocelot are still known to exist in the state, with the mountain lion and bobcat being the only species legally hunted.

Jaguar
Panthera onca

> *Col. C. of Texas told me that on the Benard River while he was hunting coons with a friend, the dogs treed something in an immense live oak, over which they made an unusual commotion. Being the youngest, it was his fate to climb the tree and get, as they thought, the coon down. The tree was directly on the riverbank, and its horizontal branches reached nearly across... He climbed the tree and crawled out on one of those horizontal limbs. Expecting every moment to see the coon, what should present itself, upon his rising up to look around but an immense spotted tiger with eyes 'like balls of fire.' What to do was the question. He could not back out; he dared not drop into the river, for it was full of alligators. He fell upon this plan: he swung himself below the limb and hung on by his hands! The tiger walked over him, descended the tree, and went through a crowd of nine dogs—as fierce ones as there were in Texas— which never even growled at him.*
>
> — Capt. William Seaton Henry, 1847

The jaguar's history in Texas is scattered and, much like the cat itself, often mysterious. Called a tiger, *el tigre*, or leopard by early Anglo settlers, the jaguar once held dominion over the majority of the state. Despite its shy and reclusive manner, jaguars are formable hunters able to take prey as large as longhorn cattle.

Although thought to be completely extinct in Texas, new sightings of jaguar in Arizona, thought to have migrated from Mexico, give experts hope that *el tigre* could possibly return in the future.

Terror in the Night

Each day's end brought fear and a sense of unease to the small ranching community of Center City, Texas, in the fall of 1903. For weeks, haunting shrieks cut the night's silence, awakening ranchers in the dead hours long before dawn. Watchdogs barked incessantly either in warning or in fear at the unidentified noises and stock began disappearing almost nightly. At first, only smaller animals such as sheep and goats turned up missing, but over time the animals that went missing got larger. Even cows started to disappear. Of the few animal remains that were found, ranchers agreed that they were all slain in the same manner and that whatever was doing the killing was extremely large and very strong.

One morning a few ranchers with their watchdogs in tow came upon a slain cow at the edge of some woods. The dogs began barking feverishly at something unseen within the trees. As the men rode the edge of the motte, a dark shape flew from the ground almost straight up into the trees, disappearing into the thick foliage.

By the time the story got around town, the unknown and still almost unseen animal had gotten bigger and bigger. Exaggeration fueled fear, and people began to wonder aloud what had all but taken control of the night. Most of the old-timers were convinced that it could only be a mountain lion. But skeptics said that a mountain lion couldn't be that large and not nearly that strong.

As the story circulated, ranchers discovered another slaughtered animal. This time it was a huge longhorn. Although some argued that it appeared the animal could have died from natural causes, most believed that it was killed by the same phantom that had been stalking the area for weeks. Fueling that theory was the torn earth surrounding the fallen longhorn that, to some, indicated a violent struggle. Although all involved were uncertain as to what they were dealing with, most agreed that it was time for action.

The call was put out for trail hounds and any man with a gun and courage enough to ride after the stock killer. Hunters and their dogs from all over Mills County answered the call, and it wasn't long before the dogs picked up the scent.

Close to dusk on September 3, 1903, Henry Morris, Homer Brown and John Walton were the first group to pick up the scent. Their dogs trailed furiously, leading the men to the edge of a thick stand of shin oaks. The hunters peered into the curtain of underbrush for signs of the animal but could only make out a set of glowing eyes peering back at them. At the dog's charge, the concealed beast let out a blood-curdling scream causing the pack to turn and run from the woods. The hunters frantically tried unsuccessfully to coax the dogs back into the thicket to corner the animal or possibly flush it into the open.

As the dogs entered the brush again, an immense paw suddenly latched onto Jack, Homer Brown's Beagle Redbone Cross Hound and pulled it from the rest of the pack. In a violent blur the animal grabbed Jack in its jaws, crushed his skull and flung his dead body aside. Unfazed by the attack, the dogs continued all efforts to subdue the animal

Morris, deciding that they would need heavier ammunition and the help of others, rode off, leaving Brown, Walton and the dogs to keep the animal at bay. It didn't take long for the others to arrive and see the commotion firsthand.

Dogs that got close to the edge of the thicket were swiped at. Those that ventured too close were cut to ribbons and thrown aside by the still totally unseen animal. The night air was filled with the screams of dogs and the rapid volley of gunshots in haste or in fear.

The Mills County Jaguar

Suddenly, and without warning, the cornered animal bolted from its surroundings. Hunters saw a blur of motion with the remaining dogs giving chase. The pack ran the animal up a small Spanish oak in the middle of another thicket. Brown rode within shooting range and fired his shotgun at the huge animal hitting it in the hip. The beast fell to the ground and the remaining pack swarmed on top of it. The dogs' barks immediately changed to screams and yelps as the pile of writhing animals exploded. Dogs were slashed open and thrown, some a distance of 20 feet or more, to their death. Then, just as suddenly as it had done before, the ferocious beast broke free from the few remaining dogs and ran into thicker cover.

Old Red, one of Claude Eacott's dogs, badly ripped open across his shoulders and one of the few dogs left alive, hobbled after the beast. The hunters chased after the animal until it was cornered once more. The only thing separating the men from the beast was one or two dogs and a few small bushes. One of the hunters decided that he would charge the animal and finish him off. He dug his spurs into his horse's sides and charged forward.

As the mounted horse jumped the small bush, the beast on the other side sprung forward to meet the challenge. The animal caught the horse in the hindquarters, immediately sinking its teeth and claws into the meat of the leg. The horse collapsed with the rider atop him screaming, "Don't shoot...you might hit me or the horse!"

Eacott, fearing for the trapped hunter's life, dug his spurs into his own horse, charging into the violent exchange. The animal turned loose of the first horse and lunged at Eacott, coming within inches of his head. As the beast hit the ground, Eacott turned and fired another shotgun blast into the animal that ran free from the commotion before collapsing.

The hunters collected the beast and took him back to town for all to see. It wasn't until they were back in Center City that the animal was identified as a jaguar. The huge male weighed 152 pounds and had a foreleg that was 21 inches around. The cat had killed countless stock animals and on the night of the hunt, it killed eight dogs and injured numerous others. Before being mounted and displayed in a museum in Austin, the jaguar was scored by the Boone and Crockett Club, which, to this day, still lists the animal as one of the largest taken in North America.

—*Portions of this piece first appeared in* Sporting Classics Magazine.

Jaguarondi
Felis yagouaroundi

Preferring the same type of thick cover in South Texas as ocelots, the jaguarondi is a long, slender cat not much larger than a house cat. Jaguarondis are dark grayish to blackish red and resemble the weasel in appearance. They eat such small animals as mice, rats and rabbits as well as birds. Extremely good jumpers, jaguarondis have been seen in the wild jumping nearly 5 feet into the air to snag a low-flying bird. Much like the ocelot, the chances of seeing jaguarondis in the wild are extremely slim. Jaguarondis are listed as endangered in Texas.

*A jaguarondi found dead on
a highway near Harlingen.*

Margay
Felis wiedii

Similar in appearance to ocelots, margays are thought to be extinct in Texas with the last sighting reported in 1850. Once roaming throughout southern Texas, margays are now limited to the area between Northern Mexico and Argentina.

Ocelot
Felis pardalis

> *One of the most common of the cat family, found in almost all river bottoms, is the beautifully spotted leopard cat, whose fur makes a fine flap for a hunting bag.*
>
> —Viktor Bracht, 1848

Looking like the jaguar's smaller cousin, the ocelot is a small, spotted cat about the size of a bobcat. Specimens average anywhere from 22 to 34 pounds. Historically known as a leopard cat or *el tigre chiquito,* ocelots once roamed throughout the southern two-thirds of the state.

Today it is only found in a few counties in the South Texas Plains and Gulf Prairies and Marshes regions.

The ocelot's diet mainly consists of smaller animals such as mice, rabbits, rats, birds, reptiles and fish. Larger game such as piglets and lambs are also occasionally taken.

Due to the ocelot's secretive ways and the fact that it inhabits only the thickest of cover, the chances of seeing an ocelot in the wild are extremely slim. Ocelots are listed as endangered in Texas.

Ocelot taken in Cameron County, circa 1924.

WOLVES

Red Wolf
Canis rufus

Gray Wolf
Canis lupus

> *Nothing occurred worthy of mention, except that we saw a great number of wolves, which had surrounded a small herd of buffalo cows and calves, and killed and eaten several. We dispersed them by firing on them. We judged, that there were at least a thousand. They were large and as white as sheep.*
> — James Ohio Pattie, 1833

> *The wolves here are as numerous as people in Germany. Any hour of the day you would meet a pack of from 200 to 300, and when night came they howled so no one could sleep.*
> — Carl Hilmar Guenther, 1851

> *Every part of Texas has wolves in smaller or greater abundance, and I think that there are not less than six different kinds...At night they approach in large packs near towns, close to the house...*
> — Viktor Bracht, 1848

Once one of the most numerous predators in the state, wolves have been eradicated from Texas since the 1960s. State and federal government programs as well as sheep and cattle ranchers either poisoned, shot or trapped gray and red wolves into extinction in Texas and the rest of the lower 48.

In Texas, the gray wolf is being bred at Fossil Rim in Glenn Rose, Texas, with much success although there are no plans to reintroduce them into the wild anytime soon.

4

Small Game & Furbearers

Due to the number of animals, varied habitat of the species and generous bag limits, the small game of Texas offers hunters the most opportunities for going afield in the Lone Star State. Much like with predatory game, not all of the animals in this chapter are regulated as game animals by Texas Parks and Wildlife. Some are considered non-game, while others are considered furbearers. Some are regulated by season in some counties while in other parts of the state they have no regulation whatsoever. And some animals need a specific license to trap but not to harvest.

Regardless of classification, all of the animals in this chapter offer hunters the opportunity for a great time.

Armadillo
Dasypus novemcinctus

Affectionately referred to as a Texas speed bump or as a "possum on the half-shell" due to its frequency of being found squished on Texas highways (possums unofficially rank first in road kill), the nine-banded armadillo has a love-hate relationship with the citizens of Texas. Despite the fact that no one likes it digging in their yard, the armadillo has been appointed as the official state mammal (small).

While some are fearful of the 'dillo's undeserved reputation as a carrier of leprosy, armadillos can be found racing before cheering fans in county fairs across the state. Love them or hate them, due to the armadillo's meager environmental requirements and high adaptability, it can be found throughout the state (except in some extreme far western counties) and it isn't going anywhere.

Averaging 29 inches from snout to tail and weighing between 11 and 17 pounds, the nine-banded armadillo is unlike any other animal in Texas. In fact, the armadillo is the only member of the scientific order *Xenarthra* found in the United States. The order's other members (sloth and other species of armadillos) are restricted to Central and South America.

Armadillos are covered from neck to rump with a hard, bone like carapace in the shape of a nine-sectioned accordion. When threatened or cornered the animal can "roll" into their shell, forming a semi-ball. Aside from fleeing, this is the animal's only means of protection as its formidable claws are designed for digging rather than self defense. Despite looking like armored tanks, armadillos can swim but often times walk on the bottom of bodies of water rather than do so.

Armadillos have an extremely varied diet, eating everything from insects, reptiles, eggs and grubs to invertebrates, worms, crawfish and carrion. This fondness for subterranean food often leads to problems with suburban dwellers mindful of their flower gardens and lawn.

Often called "the poor man's pork," armadillo meat is considered similar in taste and texture to pork and is frequently eaten in Mexico and parts of Texas. Armadillos are classified as a non-game animal in Texas.

Best Places to Hunt: Armadillos are found throughout the state except in a few western counties of the Trans-Pecos Mountains and Basins region.

Recommended Calibers: Although a few old-timers swear by the use of a bat or club, .22 Mag. or .22 Hornet offers a good backup plan.

Road kill

While living in a state that has more deer than any other in the union might be a hunter's dream, it is certainly the nightmare of many auto-insurance agents. Everyday a wide assortment of fauna can be found dead and in various states of flattened conditions on Texas roadways. Some animals, such as rabbits, squirrels and possums, cause very little damage to vehicles when hit. Others, such as boar, exotics and buzzards can all but destroy a car on impact and even send drivers to the hospital or morgue. But of all the animals motorists meet upon the blacktop, deer are by far the most numerous and most costly.

In certain parts of Texas, hitting a deer with your vehicle at some point is inevitable. Collisions between cars and deer are so numerous that according to the Insurance Institute for Highway Safety (IIHS), Texas leads the nation in numbers of vehicle-deer crashes per year, an honor the state has held since 2000. While the number of accidents varies year to year (authorities admit the yearly numbers are probably much higher as not all crashes are reported), one need only look to Kerr County to get an understanding of just how bad the problem can be.

In 2005, the Kerr County District Office of the Texas Department of Transportation reported that employees removed more than 1,500 dead deer alone from the county's roadways. And again, this number reflects deer only (numbers for other road kill workers pick up aren't kept). As some say, hitting a deer in Texas isn't a matter of "if" but rather a matter of "when," and motorists should heed the following tips.

- Use extra caution when driving at dawn, dusk and nighttime, as these are the most active times for deer on the road.
- Use headlight high beams (if possible, don't blind other drivers) to help spot deer "eye reflections" on the side of the road.
- Reduce speed when deer are spotted.
- Do not swerve, veer off the road or steer into other lanes to avoid hitting deer. If an impact is unavoidable, hold the steering wheel tight and drive straight forward.
- After impact, move to the road's shoulder to assess damage and contact local authorities for assistance if needed.

Badger
Taxidea taxus

The Mexican Badger, the body of which will weigh about forty pounds, of a brindled color and made fight with the energy of a Tiger.

— Brad C. Fowler, 1853

Despite being grammatically challenged, Brad C. Fowler was correct in his assertion of the badger's tenacity. When cornered, badgers will take on any threat, regardless of its size, with a ferocity almost unmatched in the animal kingdom. Badgers have been known to take on dogs, coyotes, snakes, horses and anything else that challenges them.

A burrowing animal weighing between 8 and 20 pounds and reaching 28 inches in length, the American (or as Fowler noted, Mexican) badger is a short, stout member of the weasel family. With long front claws, badgers can dig at unequaled rates in pursuit of food or shelter.

Badgers are gray with a white stripe running the length of the back with white areas on the face, neck and ears. The underbelly is also whitish to yellow. The feet and parts of the head are black. Badgers are found throughout Texas with the exception of the eastern most Pineywoods.

Badgers are diggers at heart and will eat almost any animal it can catch or dig up. Their diet includes rabbits, ground squirrels, rats, lizards, insects, eggs and carrion. Despite being classified as furbearers in Texas, badger fur is of little value.

Best Places to Hunt: Badgers are found throughout Texas with the exception of the easternmost border.

Recommended Calibers: Most badgers are taken by opportunistic hunters in search of other game. For those actively seeking badger, .22 Mag. or .22 Hornet are recommended.

Beaver
Castor Canadensis

Having the distinction of being the largest rodent in Texas, the American beaver can reach weights in excess of 60 pounds and measure more than 45 inches in length. Beavers are extremely well suited to their aquatic environment, having webbed rear feet and especially thick, lush insulating fur. This fur, which is chestnut to dark brown, almost meant extinction for beavers as they were heavily trapped throughout the United States without regulation until 1910. Having rebounded tremendously since earning protection and well-regulated trapping seasons, today beavers are found throughout the majority of Texas with the exception of the Llano Estacado and sections of the Trans-Pecos Mountains and Basins region.

Beavers are similar to man in the fact that they have the ability to manipulate and control their environment. By building dams, beavers create an environment that better suits their needs. When the area becomes unsuitable due to the build up of silt, the animal simply moves to another area.

In colder regions, beavers construct homes from sticks, debris and mud. These homes are generally accessible only through underwater tunnels called "plunge holes." In Texas, however, burrows are utilized as shelter and as a place to rear young (kits). Beavers are social animals often living in colonies of six or more animals.

The beaver's diet includes a wide variety of grasses, cattails, lilies, bark and other plant matter.

Beavers are listed as furbearers in Texas and are heavily trapped for their pelts. In East Texas, many trappers and hunters swear by the beaver's lean red meat. The beaver's flat, skillet shaped tail is said to harbor extremely tender meat as well.

Best Places to Hunt: Beavers are found throughout the state with the exception of some areas of the Llano Estacado and Trans-Pecos Mountains and Basins region.

Recommended Calibers: .22 Mag., .22 Hornet, .222 and .223 are used.

GROUND SQUIRRELS

There are five species of ground squirrel residing in Texas and with the exception of the rock squirrel, all are extremely small in size and weight. Most weigh less than a pound. All species are classified as non-game animals by Texas Parks and Wildlife and all generally require extreme patience and long shots from hunters due to the animal's fleeting speed and constantly moving manner.

Texas Antelope Squirrel
Ammospermophilus interpres

The Texas antelope squirrel is found only in the Trans-Pecos Mountains and Basins and the extreme southwest of the Edwards Plateau regions of the state. It lives in rocky, uneven terrain and seems to avoid the more level and sandy areas altogether. It is a small animal, weighing less than a pound and measuring less than 9 inches long.

Texas antelope squirrels are light to sandy brown with two white stripes running the length of the back. The underbelly and area around the eyes are white to gray.

In addition to digging their own burrows, Texas antelope squirrels will inhabit the abandoned burrows of other animals so long as they present a safe place to live. Most daylight hours are spent foraging above ground looking for the seeds and fruit that make up the bulk of their diet.

Mexican Ground Squirrel
Spermophilus mexicanus

Inhabiting the western two-thirds of the state minus the upper Panhandle, the Mexican ground squirrel is slightly larger than its Texas antelope squirrel cousin. It is also more attractive, having a bushy, brown coat marked with nine rows of white spots. Underbelly and sides are white to pink with the long, dark brown tail. In some ways, this squirrel's pelt resembles that of an axis deer.

Mexican ground squirrels are omnivores. In addition to eating various leaves and berries, it will also eat insects and carrion. The animal lives in dug burrows and hibernates during winter.

Spotted Ground Squirrel
Spermophilus spilosoma

Just as its name implies, the spotted ground squirrel is covered in light spots. Unlike the Mexican ground squirrel, the spotted ground squirrel's spots are more or less scattered over its grayish brown fur rather than in rows.

Spotted ground squirrels inhabit the western third of Texas minus the bulk of the Edward Plateau vegetational region. Their diet consists of seeds, beans, gourds and cactus pulp as well as insects. They live in burrows and are most active early in the morning and late in the afternoon.

Thirteen-lined Ground Squirrel
Spermophilus tridecemlineatus

The thirteen-lined ground squirrel is a grayish to brown squirrel with 13 rows of alternating light and dark stripes running the length of its back. The animal's light stripes tend to fade into spots toward the rear of the animal while dark stripes are intermittently spotted with light spots.

The animal's range in Texas gerrymanders from the Panhandle, along the northeastern state line, before turning southward and running in a narrow strip to the Gulf Coastal Plains and Marshes. The preferred habitat is grasslands, but it has little trouble in adapting to pastures.

The thirteen-lined ground squirrel has a varied diet that includes grasses, herbs, seeds, flowers and insects. The Rip Van Winkle of ground squirrels, this species hibernates roughly 240 days a year.

Rock Squirrel
Spermophilus variegatus

Averaging slightly under 2 pounds and around 1 foot in length, rock squirrels are considerably larger than the other species of ground squirrels found in Texas. Looking more like a tree squirrel than their smaller brethren, rock squirrels are either dark brown or black with white undersides. Their tails are bushy and contain a mixture of light gray and dark fur. They are found primarily in the Trans-Pecos Mountains and Basins and Edwards Plateau regions of the state.

Rock squirrels are excellent climbers and often reside on steep, rocky cliffs. In higher elevations, such as in the Guadalupe Mountains, rock squirrels have been known to climb and live in trees. On the ground, they den in rock crevices or in boulder piles.

In addition to eating such plant material as acorns, nuts, mesquite seeds, berries and gourds, rock squirrels also eat a variety of insects. They are also fond of catching and eating small birds.

Like most ground squirrels, rock squirrels are very wary of humans and are especially fast, thus the appeal for those who utilize them as long distance targets.

Best Places to Hunt: Most of the Texas ground squirrels reside in the western half of the state.

Recommended Calibers: Ground squirrels are shot with anything and everything. Those hunting close to their quarry opt for .17, .22 Mag. or .22 Hornet. Those wanting to try them from far distances choose everything from .223, 6 PPC, all the way up to .50 caliber.

Mink
Mustela vison

Mink are a long, slender, weasel-like, semi aquatic carnivore averaging between 2 and 3 pounds and measuring slightly less than 2 feet. Their fur is dark brown to black with darker areas on upper back and tail. The feet and the end of the tail are almost black while there is a small white strip running the length of the underbelly.

Living in the eastern one-third of the state, mink are found in streams, marshes, rivers and lakes. Despite their small size, mink are excellent hunters and are more than capable of killing much larger animals, such as the muskrat, which mink will often kill in order to obtain a free den.

The mink diet consists of frogs, fish, clams, mussels, snakes, muskrats and other small animals. Birds and carrion are also eaten.

Due in part to commercial mink farms, wild mink fur is not in as high demand as it once was in Texas. Minks are classified as furbearers in Texas.

Best Places to Hunt: Mink are found in the eastern half of the state.

Recommended Calibers: .17, .22, .22 Mag. and .22 Hornet are used.

Muskrat
Ondatra zibethicus

The common muskrat is a fairly large aquatic rodent averaging 20 inches in length and weighing slightly more than 2 pounds. It is dark brown to black with a small white patch beneath the chin. Its long, scaly rat-like tail easily accounts for half the animal's total length. Rear feet are partially webbed. Muskrat habitat is scattered throughout Texas but for the most part consists of the extreme eastern portion of the state, along the Louisiana border, in the northern Panhandle and a few isolated areas of West Texas.

Muskrats eat a variety of plants and grasses but will turn to carrion or cannibalism when food sources become scarce. This is especially true during harsh winters.

Similar to beavers, muskrats live in dome-shaped homes constructed from cut vegetation and debris or in burrowed dens.

Although once the most economically important and sought after furbearer in the state, the muskrat has fallen victim to changes in the fur market, loss of habitat and direct competition with the much larger nutria.

Best Places to Hunt: Muskrats inhabit the northeastern, southwestern and southeastern portions of the state.

Recommended Calibers: .22 Mag., .22 Hornet, .222, .223 are used.

Nutria
Myocastor coypus

Nutrias first began wreaking havoc on the United States in 1940 when roughly 150 of the animals escaped from a private reserve in Louisiana owned by Tabasco sauce founder L. E. McIlhenny. In the decades since their accidental release, nutria have spread across the eastern two-thirds of Texas as well as a large portion of the southern United States.

Originally from South America, the nutria is a beaver-sized rodent measuring upwards of 2 feet in length and tipping the scales at more than 20 pounds. They are reddish brown with a small grayish white patch under the chin. The animal's always-growing incisors are bright orange. The tail is long, scaly and rat-like. The hind feet are webbed.

Equally at home in salt or freshwater, nutria inhabit the majority of waterways, lakes, ponds and estuaries throughout the central and eastern portion of the state. The nutria diet consists of a variety of plants, grasses and reeds. They will also eat shellfish.

Nutria are extremely prolific, reaching sexual maturity at five months. The average litter size is five but can go as high as 11. This constantly expanding population when combined with the animal's insatiable appetite give good insight into why nutria are such unwanted and loathed pests.

In efforts to attract more hunters and trappers to the nutria dilemma in Louisiana, restaurant chefs were employed to create culinary masterpieces with nutria meat. Unsurprisingly, this program met with little success. Despite the fact that nutria meat is said to be excellent table fare, few restaurant diners lined up to eat what appears to be a large rat.

Although not indigenous to the state, nutria are classified as furbearers in Texas.

Best Places to Hunt: Nutria have taken over most bodies of water in the eastern two-thirds of the state.

Recommended Calibers: .22 Mag., .22 Hornet, .222, .223 are used.

Opossum or Possum
Didelphis virginiana

… Their flesh is much like Pig.

— Henri Joutel, 1687

Aside from having the distinction of being the only marsupial native to North America, the Virginia opossum has very little else going for it. It is by far the ugliest animal in the state, the most common animal found dead on Texas highways, and one of the most despised animals by homeowners due to its love of nesting in attics and eating out of trashcans. Despite its lack of popularity, the possum is probably one of the most successful animals in the state. It is at home in the city and suburbs as well as in the wild and, aside from a few desert areas in West Texas, is found throughout the state.

Looking like a large grayish white rat with a pink snout and pink feet, the possum averages 30 inches in length and can weigh upwards of 10 pounds. The tail is long, rat-like and free from long hairs. Possums are relatively slow on the ground and this, combined with their occasional defense mechanism of playing dead, accounts for their numerous deaths on public roads. Although nocturnal in nature, possums are occasionally seen during daylight hours.

The possum diet is varied and includes just about anything they can find, catch, scavenge or kill. Possums eat insects, fish, mollusks, small reptiles, frogs, small mammals, carrion, animal feeds, crops, fruits, berries and vegetables.

Possums tend to live in hollow trees, rock crevices, caves and abandoned burrows or dens. In proximity to man, they will use attics, wood piles, sheds and building overhangs.

Although classified as furbearers in Texas, possums have very little commercial value in the fur trade. Despite the stigma, possum meat is said to be quite good.

Best Places to Hunt: Opossums are found throughout the state with the exception of a few counties in the Trans-Pecos Mountains and Basins region.

Recommended Calibers: .22 Mag. or .22 Hornet.

Itch Like the Devil

Years of hunting have taken me to some of the vilest and most inhospitable places on earth. I've crawled through the chest-deep muck of the Texas coastal marshes in search of trophy alligator, accompanied an entomologist into the dank, sunless rainforests of Papua New Guinea in pursuit of the elusive cassowary bird and crawled on hands and knees through an impenetrable tapestry of thorns and briars for a better shot at a massive kudu in South Africa without any serious mishap, illness or injury. With such experiences under my belt, I didn't think twice about shooting a possum that had made his home in an old barn on my friend's deer lease.

Author Gayne C. Young and the source of his itching.

After a quick shot to his head, I pulled the pouched rat out from under piles of lumber and crates and buried him. The next morning my midsection was covered with tiny red bumps and itched like the devil. As the day progressed, the itching got worse. By the next morning, my midsection looked like a cheese grater had attacked me. A trip to the doctor quickly revealed the cause of my ailment.

"How did you get possum scabies?" John Ramsey, my family physician, asked with a wicked smile.

After going through the traumatic event once more, Dr. Ramsey explained the ins and outs of *Sarcoptes scabiei*.

Scabies are tiny mites that live and feed within the flesh of their host. The nonhuman type of scabies generally have no interest in humans unless there is no other food source available. Scabies are often found in abandoned buildings, chicken coups and barns where they lay in wait for the next free meal.

Possum, or varmint scabies, are unable to live in humans very long but make the most out of the time they do. Although they burrow and feed under the skin, it is their excrement that is deposited under the skin that causes an itchy reaction. Treatment is in the form of a prescribed cream and takes less than 24 hours to work.

The best way to avoid scabies is to avoid the dank, deserted places in which they live. To remove the threat, buildings should be aired out regularly. A spray mixture of one cup of bleach to one gallon of water will destroy any infestation. Hunters and trappers run little risk of infestation so long as they take such precautionary measures as wearing gloves (and not hunting in abandoned buildings).

Although I can now look back upon my days as being a host for hundreds of parasitic mites with a sense of humor, at the time it was one of the most uncomfortable experiences of my life. I truly itched like the devil.

Otter
Lutra Canadensis

Widely known for their playful antics, otters are large, slender, weasel-like, aquatic animals averaging a little more than 3 feet in length and occasionally tipping the scales at more than 20 pounds. They are remarkable swimmers with webbed feet and a thick, powerful tail. They are dark brown and their fur has a glossy sheen.

Otters are found in rivers, lakes, streams and marshes throughout the eastern quarter of the state and in brackish inlets and pools along the Gulf Coast. Their diet consists of fish, crustaceans, mollusks, small reptiles, amphibians, birds and small mammals. Although seemingly cute in nature, otters are fearsome fighters and will often kill muskrats or beavers in order to take over their dens.

Otters are classified as furbearers in Texas. A CITES tag is required if the pelt is to be sold or shipped out of state.

Best Places to Hunt: Otters are found throughout the eastern half of the state.

Recommended Calibers: .22 Mag., .22 Hornet.

Porcupine
Erethizon dorsatum

Running a close second behind the armadillo in terms of odd appearances, the porcupine is a large, quill-covered rodent averaging between 11 and 24 pounds in weight and reaching roughly 2 feet in length. They are yellowish brown in appearance due in part to yellow colored guard hairs that extend beyond the animal's whitish brown quills. These guard hairs also help make the animal appear larger than it actually is as well as contributing to the animal's rounded, butterball appearance. Porcupines are primarily found in the western half of the state.

Porcupines are herbivores, with ground vegetation and tree bark making up the bulk of their diet. They are also extremely fond of salt and will often spend considerable time enjoying salt licks and mineral blocks put out by ranchers for cattle or deer.

Although slow moving on the ground, porcupines are expert climbers and are capable of scaling rocks and trees with ease. They den in caves, rock overhangs or rock crevices.

Porcupines are listed as non-game animals in Texas.

Best Places to Hunt: Porcupines are found in the western half of the state.

Recommended Calibers: .22 Mag. and .22 Hornet.

Prairie Dogs
Cynomys ludovicianus

Correctly identified as the black-tailed prairie dog, this large member of the ground squirrel family averages a little more than a foot long and between 2 to 4 pounds in weight. It is light brown in appearance with a short black-tipped tail.

Prairie dogs are social animals and live in "towns" made up of connected tunnels. Historically, these towns, and the prairie dogs themselves, were found throughout the western half of the state. Towns spreading for several square miles and consisting of hundreds to thousands of animals were not uncommon. Today the animal's range has shrunk considerably.

Like most rodents, prairie dogs have a voracious appetite and at times seem capable of eating almost nonstop. It is estimated that 32 prairie dogs will consume as much food in one day as will an adult sheep.

The prairie dog's diet consists of a number of weeds, grasses and prickly pear. In the past, prairie dogs were the subjects of many eradication programs. Today, however, scientists and ranchers are discovering that in areas were prairie dogs have been removed, brush has reappeared and spread quickly.

Best Places to Hunt: Prairie dogs are found in the western half of the state.

Recommended Calibers: Prairie dogs are often taken at incredible distances. Hunters opt for anything between the .223 and .50 caliber.

RABBITS

There are four species of rabbit residing in Texas, and, due to their prolific nature, all are quite common.

Despite being called a rabbit, the swamp rabbit is considered a cottontail. It, along with the desert and eastern cottontail, compromise the three species of cottontail in the state. All are relatively small, extremely quick, seek shelter in dense undergrowth and have a fluffy white tail that resembles a ball of cotton. They are also the most common of the Texas rabbits hunted for food.

Although hunted extensively, the black-tailed jackrabbit is generally hunted for sport rather than food.

Swamp Rabbit
Sylvilagus aquaticus

Found in the eastern one-third of the state, the swamp rabbit is considered to be the largest of the cottontails. It averages between 3 to 7 pounds and reaches lengths up to 21 inches. As the name implies, it inhabits swamp and marsh

areas as well as river bottoms. Its grayish brown coat of dense fur helps protect and waterproof its skin when crossing bodies of water or in inclement weather.

Like most rabbits it is extremely quick and often takes shelter in the thickest of cover. Its diet includes grasses, shoots, forbs and other plant material.

Desert Cottontail
Sylvilagus audubonii

Similar in appearance but smaller in size than its swamp-dwelling cousin, the desert cottontail averages between 1 to 3 pounds and reaches 16 inches in length. It is found in a variety of habitats in the western half of the state. In the plains regions, it is often found in the proximity of prairie dog towns and is thusly referred to as the prairie-dog rabbit.

In addition to eating a variety of grasses and leaves, seedpods, prickly pear, twigs and bark are also part of their diet.

Eastern Cottontail
Sylvilagus floridanus

Aside from being slightly smaller in size and having smaller ears, the eastern cottontail is almost the spitting image of its desert counterpart. The eastern cottontail is found throughout the state, in all types of environments, and is the most common rabbit in Texas as well as in the United States.

Twigs and bark make up part of the animals diet when grasses and forbs are scarce.

Black-tailed Jackrabbit
Lepus californicus

*When the plains have become settled and civilized, and the
large game killed off, he [jackrabbit] will furnish to the sportsman an unfailing source of pleasure, and I doubt not the time
will come when coursing this animal will be as common here as
coursing the hare in England.*

— Richard Irving Dodge, 1877

Although generally associated with the arid, western section of the
state, the black-tailed jackrabbit (also called jackrabbit or jackass rabbit) is found throughout Texas with the exception of a few counties
in the extreme southeastern corner of the state. It is a large rabbit, averaging 23 inches in length and pushing close to 9 pounds in weight.
Its coat is grayish brown with a whitish underside. The tips of ears,
tail and hindquarters are black.

Unlike other rabbits in Texas, the jackrabbit has extremely long ears, averaging 6 inches in length. These not only help in detecting the slightest noise, but also serve as a way to release excess body heat.

When threatened or disturbed, the jackrabbit generally freezes in place, hoping to blend into its surroundings. If pushed, however, it is capable of reaching speeds of up to 35 miles per hour. This speed, when combined with the rabbit's zigzag running style, makes it an extremely elusive animal.

The jackrabbit's diet consists of grasses, herbs, leaves and crops as well as supplemental foods put out for other animals. Although not as commonly eaten as other rabbit species, those who are fond of jackrabbit swear by it.

Best Places to Hunt: Swamp rabbits are found in the eastern one-third of the state. Eastern cottontails are found in the eastern portion of the state. Desert cottontails are found in the western half of state. Jackrabbits are found throughout the state with the exception of the extreme eastern border of the state.

Recommended Calibers: .17, .22, .22 Mag., .22 Hornet are recommended or shotgun #4 or #6 pellets.

———————————

Raccoon
Procyon lotor

The raccoon is the size of a badger—gray brown with a white nose and a brown stripe over the eyes. There are five black stripes on the eight-to-ten-inch long tail.

— Friederich W. von Wrede, 1838

Walker had provided again for a roast on the way. The bullet of his good gun had killed a raccoon, which, spread out on poles like a bat, was roasted on the fire.

— *Gustav Dresel, 1839*

Raccoons are a medium-sized carnivore averaging between 9 and 30 pounds in weight and reaching 34 inches in length. Its coat is a mix of grayish-silver and black. It has a bushy tail with alternating brown and black stripes, wears a black bandit mask across the face and thanks to the legend of Davy Crockett is probably the only animal in Texas ever mistaken for a hat.

The common or northern raccoon (also called mapache) occurs throughout the state, inhabiting every conceivable type of terrain. They are as at home in the city and suburbs as they are in their intended and natural habitat. In the wild, they reside in hollow trees, caves, rock jumbles or deep crevices. Closer to man, they will take up residence in outbuildings, attics or building overhangs.

The raccoon's diet consists of berries, fruits, insects, crustaceans, mollusks, fish, birds and snakes. Raccoons are also fond of agricultural crops, gardens, cattle feed and anything coming out of a deer feeder.

Raccoons have long been hunted at night with dogs, but due to ever shrinking wild areas, this practice is not as common as it once was. Today most raccoons are hunted at night with a spotlight or by calling. In Texas, raccoons are listed as furbearers and are one of the more sought after members of this group.

Best Places to Hunt: Raccoons are found statewide.

Recommended Calibers: .22 Mag., .22 Hornet, .222, .223 are recommended or shotgun #4 or #6 pellets.

Ringtail
Bassariscus astutus

> *It is a lively, playful and nimble creature, leaps about on the*
> *trees, and has very much the same actions as the squirrel...*
> — Dr. Ferdinand Roemer, 1849

Looking like a cross between a fox, cat and raccoon, the ringtail, or ring-tailed cat, is a small carnivore averaging between 2 and 3 pounds and reaching 31 inches in length. They are grayish with a long, bushy tail striped in alternating black and white rings. This "ringed tail" is more than half the animal's length. The eyes are masked in white.

Ringtails (also called cacomistle) are found throughout the state but are more common in the Edwards Plateau and Trans-Pecos Mountains and Basins region. They are expert climbers and prefer to den in rocky areas.

Despite the animal's cute appearance and small size, ringtails are excellent hunters and are easily capable of killing rabbits, squirrels, rats, mice and birds for food. Snakes, lizards, frogs, toads and native fruits are also eaten.

Ringtails are listed as furbearers in Texas.

Best Places to Hunt: Ringtails are found throughout the state but are rare along the coast and along the lower Rio Grande.

Recommended Calibers: Either .17 or .22 calibers are recommended.

SKUNKS

The skunk is commonly eaten by the soldiers and residents of the presidios in spite of its disagreeable odor. After carefully removing the anal glands and burning off its fur, the Comanches eat it with relish.

—Jean Louis Berlandier, 1828

The French people who were with us caught it, and ate it. The odor, however, was too pungent to suit everyone's olfactories.

—Lt. J. W. Abert, 1845

Striped skunk

There are six species of skunk residing in Texas and all of them possess the defense mechanism for which they are famous. All are black in color with some form of distinctive white markings along the back.

All species are predominantly nocturnal but will occasionally venture out in daylight to hunt or if disturbed. Although skunks are in no way related to the European, weasel-like polecat, they are often called polecats in Texas.

Western Spotted Skunk
Spilogale gracilis

Weighing less than 2 pounds and averaging 17 inches in length, the western spotted skunk is by far the most flamboyantly decorated member of the skunk family found in Texas. In addition to having four white dorsal stripes that run the length of its predominantly black coat, the animal also has white cheek markings and a small white vertical stripe on the forehead. The tail resembles a Vegas showgirl's headpiece in that billowy loose plumes of white hair surround a black center.

The western spotted skunk is found throughout the South Texas Plains and Trans-Pecos Mountains and Basins region where it dens in rock jumbles, rocky bluffs and in thick brush along stream or river beds.

Its diet includes insects, scorpions, young or small mammals and eggs.

Eastern Spotted Skunk
Spilogale putorius

Similar in appearance to the western spotted skunk, the eastern spotted skunk reaches 20 inches in length and weighs less than 2 pounds. The forehead has a vertical white stripe. Large white spots are found just forward of the ears. Six white stripes are found along the back; some, such as those found on the hips, are curved while others run more or less the length of the back.

As the name implies, the eastern spotted skunk inhabits the eastern half of the state. Rock jumbles, crevices, hollow trees and outbuildings are used as den sites.

Diet is similar to other skunks and includes small mammals, insects, fruits, birds and eggs.

Hooded Skunk
Mephitis macroura

Considered to have the softest and best fur of the six species of skunks residing in Texas, the hooded skunk is found in the Trans-Pecos Mountains and Basins region where it dens in rock jumbles and in thick stream-side vegetation. It averages around 27 inches in length and weighs close to 2 pounds.

The hooded skunk is found in two color phases: the white-backed and the black-backed. As the name implies, during the white-backed phase white stripes make up the majority of the back. The opposite is true of the black-backed phase.

The hooked skunk's diet is similar to other skunks although more insects are eaten.

Striped Skunk
Mephitis mephitis

Considered a medium-sized skunk, the striped skunk averages 26 inches in length and weighs upwards of 15 pounds. The coat is black with two white stripes connected at the neck running the length of the back and occasionally down the tail. Stripes can vary considerably in size. A small, vertical white stripe runs from nose to forehead.

The striped skunk is fairly common, being found throughout the state in almost every type of environment. Its diet is similar to other skunks.

Eastern Hog-nosed Skunk
Conepatus leuconotus

Found in only a handful of counties in the Gulf Prairies and Marshes region, the eastern hog-nosed skunk is quite rare in Texas. Considered a large skunk, the eastern hog-nosed skunk averages upwards of

32 inches in length and reaches weights of more than 10 pounds. It is black with a single white stripe running the length of the back and tail. Although these markings are very close in resemblance to the common hog-nosed skunk, the eastern variety tends to have a narrower stripe.

The diet is similar to that of other skunks in Texas although more insects are eaten.

NOTE: Some people in the scientific community consider the eastern hog-nosed skunk a sub-specific variant of the common hog-nosed skunk.

Common Hog-nosed Skunk
Conepatus mesoleucus

Deriving its name from the way it roots for food, the common hog-nosed skunk (occasionally called a rooter skunk) averages around 23 inches in length and roughly 10 pounds in weight. It is black with a single white stripe running the length of the back and tail. It is predominately found in the western and central portions of the state although an isolated number of animals inhabit the eastern portion of the state as well.

Its diet is similar to that of other skunks.

Best Places to Hunt
Western spotted skunks are found in the western portion of the state. Eastern spotted skunks inhabit the eastern half of the state. Hooded skunks are found in the Big Bend area. Striped skunks are found statewide. Eastern hog-nosed skunks are scattered throughout the southern Gulf Prairies and Marshes region of the state.

Recommended Calibers: .17, .22, .22 Mag. and .22 Hornet.

SQUIRRELS

Three species of squirrel reside in Texas. All three are excellent climbers and spend the majority of their life in trees.

Eastern fox squirrel

Eastern Gray Squirrel
Sciurus carolinensis

Averaging between 18 and 19 inches in length and weighing up to 1 pound, the Eastern gray squirrel is probably the most sought after of the two game species in the state. It is so popular with hunters that the animal has been transplanted to parts of Europe to provide sporting opportunities. In Texas, however, it is found in the Eastern third of the state.

They are yellowish rust in color with softer colors or white under parts. The tail is yellowish to black and bushy.

Eastern gray squirrels den in hollow trees, but will construct a large nest if such a den is unavailable. Diet is varied and includes acorns, nuts, fungi, insects, larvae, small amphibians and crops.

Eastern Fox Squirrel
Sciurus niger

In addition to being the most common of the three species of Texas squirrels, the Eastern fox squirrel is also the largest, averaging 20 inches in length and weighing between 1 and 3 pounds in weight. It is grayish brown with rust colored under parts. The tail is less than half the body length and very bushy.

Residing in the Eastern two-thirds of the state, the Eastern fox squirrel spends the majority of its time searching for, collecting or burying food. Its diet is varied and includes acorns, nuts, fruits, seeds, and insects.

Eastern Flying Squirrel
Glaucomys volans

Averaging 9 inches in length and weighing under a half a pound, the Eastern flying squirrel is the smallest squirrel residing in Texas. Its coat is cinnamon brown with white under parts. The tail is flat but semi-bushy. A thin membrane spreading between the front and back legs allow the squirrel to glide between trees. Most glides are between 9 to 30 feet, although glides of up to 100 feet have been witnessed. The Eastern flying squirrel is found in hardwood sections of the eastern third of the state.

Unlike the other species of squirrels in Texas, the Eastern flying squirrel is mainly nocturnal. Its diet includes nuts, insects, larvae, eggs, birds and carrion.

Best Places to Hunt: Eastern fox squirrels are found in the eastern two-thirds of the state while the Eastern flying squirrel and eastern gray are restricted to the eastern third of the state.

Recommended Calibers: .17, .22, .22 Mag., .22 Hornet are recommended or a .410 shotgun with #6 pellets.

Weasel
Mustela frenata

Correctly identified as the long-tailed weasel, this species of weasel is sparsely scattered throughout the state with the exception of the upper Panhandle. It averages 19 inches in length and can weigh slightly more than one pound. It is yellowish brown with a black head, white marked face and underbelly and black tipped tail.

Despite its small size, the weasel is a ferocious hunter and slow to back down from a challenge or threat. Its diet includes ground squirrels, gophers, rats, mice, rabbits and birds. Because of its fondness for burrowing animals, the weasel is looked upon highly by farmers and ranchers.

Weasels are listed as non-game animals in Texas.

Best Places to Hunt: Weasels are found throughout the state with the exception of the Panhandle.

Recommended Calibers: .17 or .22 caliber.

HISTORIC AND ENDANGERED

Of the historic small game and furbearers of Texas, only the black-footed ferret is truly gone. The coati is still here, although not nearly as widespread as it once was. The coati is listed as threatened in Texas.

Black-footed Ferret
Mustela nigripes

Due to loss of habitat, the agricultural conversion of land, eradication programs, competition with weasels and disease, the black-footed ferret has been extinct in Texas since the early 1960s. It is federally listed as an endangered species. Reintroduction efforts in Wyoming have met with little success.

Coati
Nasua narica

With an extremely long, black ringed tail, elongated snout and dark facial band across the eyes, the coati somewhat resembles a cross between a raccoon and a ringtail. Also called the South American Coati, white-nosed coati, and coatimundi, the coati averages 44 inches in length and weighs between 8 and 11 pounds. It is yellowish brown to reddish brown with lighter colored under parts. The bottom half of its legs and feet are dark to black. It is found in the Edwards Plateau, South Texas Plains and Trans-Pecos Mountains and Basins regions of the state.

Coatis are social animals and, with the exception of older, solitary males, they live and travel in troops or packs. Unlike its cousin the raccoon, coatis are fairly active during the day and spend a great deal of time searching for food. Its diet consists of insects, lizards, snakes, small mammals, fruits, nuts, prickly pear and crops.

Coatis are listed as threatened in Texas.

5

THINGS THAT BITE

Oh, the Devil in hell they say he was chained,
And there for a thousand years he remained;
He neither complained nor did he groan,
But decided he'd start up a hell of his own,
Where he could torment the souls of men
Without being shut in a prison pen;
So he asked the Lord if He had any sand
Left over from making this great land.

The Lord He said, "Yes, I have plenty on hand,
But it's away down south on the Rio Grande,
And, to tell you the truth, the stuff is so poor
I doubt if 'twill do for hell any more."
The Devil went down and looked over the truck,
And he said if it came as a gift he was stuck,
For when he'd examined it carefully and well
He decided the place was too dry for a hell.

But the Lord just to get the stuff off His hands
He promised the Devil He'd water the land,
For he had some old water that was of no use,
A regular bog hole that stunk like the deuce.

So the grant it was made and the deed it was given;
The Lord He returned to His place up in heaven.
The Devil soon saw he had everything needed
To make up a hell and so he proceeded.

He scattered tarantulas over the roads,
Put thorns on the cactus and horns on the toads,
He sprinkled the sands with millions of ants
So the man that sits down must wear soles on his
pants.
He lengthened the horns of the Texas steer,
And added an inch to the jack rabbit's ear;
He put water puppies in all of the lakes,
And under the rocks he put rattlesnakes.

He hung thorns and brambles on all of the trees,
He mixed up the dust with jiggers and fleas;
The rattlesnake bites you, the scorpion stings,
The mosquito delights you by buzzing his wings.
The heat in the summer's a hundred and ten,
Too hot for the Devil and too hot for men;
And all who remained in that climate soon bore
Cuts, bites, stings, and scratches, and blisters galore.

— from "Hell in Texas,"
American Ballads and Folk Songs

As the song humorously brings to light, Texas is blessed with an abundance of things that either bite, cut, sting, scratch or just generally annoy. Texas is home to a multitude of poisonous plants, thorn-covered vegetation, more than 100 species of cacti, swarms of insects and more species of reptiles than any other state in the Union. Even the largest of cities aren't free from the things that bite. Fire ants, "killer bees," scourges of mosquitoes and a number of poisonous snakes have all easily adapted to and even thrive in the suburbs, greenbelts and downtown parks of Houston, Dallas, San Antonio and every other square inch of Texas that humans occupy.

Luckily, none of the aforementioned is necessarily seeking human prey. Although avoiding a painful encounter with all of the things that bite, scratch, gouge, and annoy is impossible, a little knowledge and precaution can easily keep pain and suffering to a minimum. The same holds true for the plethora of diseases and ailments that hunters are especially susceptible to when afield.

NOTE: Hunting can be very physically demanding. Traipsing through rock strewn valleys in West Texas in search of mule deer, slugging after alligator in knee-deep water or even dragging a downed buck back to camp can all definitely take a toll on the out-of-shape hunter.

In order to have a more successful and less strenuous time afield, hunters should maintain an active lifestyle throughout the year—not just in the weeks prior to a hunt. Hunters who stay in shape tend to have more energy, are more alert, tend to have better concentration and have raised immunity. Hunters should seek the advice of medical professionals before starting any new exercise program.

DANGEROUS PLANTS

Texas is a world of vegetation. From the awe-inspiring palette of spring wildflowers in the Hill Country to the sparse beauty of cactus in bloom in the Big Bend region, Texas is host to an almost countless variety of vegetation. But not all plant life in the state inspires beauty. Some, such as poison ivy, can leave those unfortunate enough to come in contact with it covered in an oozing rash that is anything but aesthetically pleasing. Others, such as mesquite and cat claw, have thorns sharp enough to puncture car tires.

Perhaps the most dangerous plants in the state are those not native to Texas. There are more than 500 species of exotic plants living in Texas. As with feral animals, the long-term effects of these plants and how they will impact the state isn't known.

As for the plants that scratch, poke, cut and infect, avoidance is always the best advice.

Contact Plants

Although any plant can cause skin irritation if the person it comes in contact with is allergic, the majority of the population feels the effects of contact with poison ivy, poison sumac and poison oak. It is estimated that more than 85 percent of the population is allergic to these three plants. Luckily, all three are easy to identify and avoid.

Poison ivy grows as either a small shrub or a vine. The leaves are clumped together in groups of three—two outer, smaller leaves and one middle longer leaf. Leaves are green in summer but may be yellow, orange or red at other times of the year.

Poison oak is similar in appearance to poison ivy with the exception of the leaves. Poison oak leaves are deeply toothed and are rounded at the tip.

Poison sumac grows as either a shrub or a tree. Leaves grow in groups of between 7 and 11 pairs with a single leaf at the end of the midrib. Yellowish green flowers and whitish berries hang from the plant in loose clusters.

These plants all produce an oily sap and when it comes in contact with a protein beneath the skin it creates an itchy rash. As the sap takes 10 to 15 minutes to penetrate the skin, the best course of action after contact is to wash the area thoroughly with soap and water. If an infection does occur, topical steroid creams and calamine-containing lotions are helpful in managing the itch.

Avoidance and long clothing are the best preventative measures.

Thorn-bearing Plants

Avoidance, heavy shoes, shin guards or gaiters and thick clothing are the best methods to evade cuts, scrapes and punctures from the many thorn-bearing plants of Texas. Areas that sustain injury should be thoroughly cleaned and treated with an antibiotic ointment such as Neosporin.

TIP: The best way to remove small needles, such as those from a cactus, is with the aid of white glue. Smear white glue over the punctured area, allow glue to dry, and pull free from skin. Needles should come out with the glue.

DISEASES, CONDITIONS AND AILMENTS

Hunting involves spending a great deal of time outdoors, often in less than stellar conditions. Time spent afield in extreme heat, cold or wet weather often following lengthy travel can lead to fatigue and a drop in immunity. When long hours, excessive food and alcohol are added to the mix, the body's natural resistance can be reduced to the breaking point. It's at these moments when ailments such as dehydration, diarrhea or exhaustion can turn the perfect hunting vacation into time spent wishing for the comforts of home. Additionally, a host of problems such as Lyme Disease, West Nile Fever and Rocky Mountain Spotted Fever lie in the mouths of insects ready to pounce.

Far less common are diseases such as Yellow Fever, malaria and plague. Although extremely rare in Texas, a basic knowledge of these diseases can help prevent infection and possibly death.

Chronic Wasting Disease

Chronic Wasting Disease, or CWD, is a fatal neurological disease found in deer and elk in some geographic locations in North America. Although there is no evidence that humans can contract Chronic Wasting Disease, either from live or dead animals or by eating an infected animal, hunters are cautioned to avoid areas of outbreaks and not to ingest any meat from an animal thought to be infected. To date, no animals in Texas with CWD have been identified.

Dehydration

Cause: Water or fluid loss is exceeded by intake
Symptoms: Thirst, fatigue, weakness, diarrhea, vomiting or fever.
Treatment: Drink water or sports drinks such as Gatorade. Severe cases should seek medical attention immediately.
Avoidance: Avoid excessive heat, drink plenty of water.

Diarrhea

Cause: Viruses, bacteria, parasites, stress, fatigue and other ailments.
Symptoms: Loose stool, abdominal cramps.
Treatment: Stay hydrated, eat bland, salty foods. Drugs such as Kaeopectate and Pepto Bismol are recommended. If the condition continues, seek medical attention.
Avoidance: Keep hydrated, wash hands frequently and shun unfamiliar foods.

Ehrlichiosis

Occurrence: Rare
Cause: Bite from an infected tick. In Texas, three species are known to carry the infection: The Lone Star tick, the blacklegged tick and the western blacklegged tick.
Symptoms: Fever, headache, fatigue, muscle aches, nausea, rash, confusion, cough or joint pain.
Treatment: Antibiotics
Avoidance: Avoid ticks and quickly remove ticks on the body. See Ticks *for additional tips.*

Heat Exhaustion

Cause: Excessive exposure to heat.

Symptoms: Heavy sweating, pale skin, weakness, dizzy, cramps, fainting, nausea or vomiting.

Treatment: Drink plenty of water or sports drinks such as Gatorade, rest, take a cool shower or bath and seek shade.

Avoidance: Avoid excessive heat and drink plenty of water.

Heat Stroke

Cause: Excessive exposure to heat.

Symptoms: Red, hot skin, temperature more than 103 degrees, rapid pulse, dizziness, confusion or fainting.

Treatment: Cool victim rapidly and seek medical attention immediately.

Avoidance: Avoid excessive heat and drink plenty of water.

Hypothermia, Frostbite

Cause: Overexposure to cold weather

Symptoms: Slurred speech, intense shivering, vision problems or low body temperature.

Treatment: Move victim to warm area, give warm liquids and seek medical attention immediately.

Avoidance: Limit time outdoors in cold weather and dress appropriately.

Lyme Disease

Occurrence: Rare

Cause: Bite from an infected tick.

Symptoms: Fever, headache, fatigue, muscle aches, nausea, cough or joint pain.

Treatment: Antibiotics

Avoidance: Avoid ticks and quickly remove attached ticks.

See Ticks *for additional tips.*

Mad Cow

Correctly identified as Bovine Spongiform Encephalopathy (BSE), Mad Cow disease is a slowly progressive, degenerative, fatal disease that affects adult cattle. The cause of the disease is unknown but the latest theories hold that the disease develops after the subject has ingested certain types of infected proteins. Mad Cow is often confused with Chronic Wasting Disease (CWD) but there is no scientific evidence that the two are related. To date no species other than cattle has contracted Mad Cow.

Malaria

Occurrence: Very rare.

Cause: Bite from an infected mosquito

Symptoms: Fever, chills, enlarged spleen, convulsions, kidney failure or hypoglycemia.

Treatment: Antibiotics.

Avoidance: Avoid mosquitoes; wear protective clothing and insect repellant.

Plague

Occurrence: Very rare. An average of 13 cases per year are reported in the United States. The last known infection in Texas was in 1993.

Cause: Bite from an infected flea. Contact with infected animal or person.

Symptoms: Fever, abdominal pain, loss of appetite, vomiting, diarrhea or gangrene.

Treatment: Antibiotics

Avoidance: Avoid fleas and dead animals, especially rabbits and rodents.

Rabies

Occurrence: Rare

Cause: Bite from an infected animal such as coyote, dogs,

raccoon, bat, opossum and others.

Symptoms: Early symptoms include abnormal muscle movement, fever or headache, malaise, nausea, sore throat and loss of appetite. Advanced symptoms include seizures, mental disturbance, paralysis and death.

Treatment: Antirabies serum.

Avoidance: Stay away from animals acting strange or unusual and wear gloves when skinning animals.

Relapsing Fever

Occurrence: Rare

Cause: Bite from infected lice or ticks.

Symptoms: Headache, muscle pain, weakness, loss of appetite, fever six days on and six days off.

Treatment: Antibiotics

Avoidance: Avoid ticks and quickly remove attached ticks. *See* Ticks *for additional tips.*

Rocky Mountain Spotted Fever

Occurrence: Rare

Cause: Bite from an infected tick.

Symptoms: Fever, headache, chills, rash on extremities, shock, delirium or kidney failure.

Treatment: Antibiotics

Avoidance: Avoid ticks and quickly remove attached ticks. *See* Ticks *for additional tips.*

Scabies

Occurrence: Fairly common. There are more than 300 million cases of scabies worldwide every year.

Cause: Mites *(Sarcoptes scabiei)* burrow beneath the skin to lay eggs. Mites do not bite, rather the itching and rash occur as a reaction to the mites' eggs and feces.

Symptoms: Intense itching, rash of raised, red bumps on the skin.

Treatment: Prescription cream.
Avoidance: Avoid infected individuals, abandoned and stagnant areas, such as old buildings, and always wear rubber gloves when skinning animals.

Sunburn

Cause: Overexposure to sun and other ultraviolet light sources.
Symptoms: Red, burning skin or blistering of skin.
Treatment: Cool bath, compress, moisturizer, aloe vera gel.
Avoidance: Avoid extended periods in strong sunlight, wear long clothing, hat and sunscreen.

Tetanus

Cause: Bacteria entering the body through broken skin.
Symptoms: Lockjaw, stiffness in abdomen and neck, difficulty swallowing followed by fever and muscle spasms.
Treatment: Clean all wounds, scrapes and cuts thoroughly. Take antibiotics.
Avoidance: Vaccinations

West Nile Virus

Occurrence: Very rare, even if bitten by an infected mosquito.
Cause: Bite from an infected mosquito.
Symptoms: Mild symptoms include fever, headache, tiredness, body aches, skin rash and swollen lymph glands. Severe symptoms include high fever, disorientation, coma, tremors, convulsions, muscle weakness and paralysis.
Treatment: Antibiotics
Avoidance: Avoid mosquitoes; wear protective clothing and insect repellant.

Yellow Fever

Occurrence: Very rare.
Cause: Bite from an infected mosquito.

Symptoms: Fever, headache, chills, rash on extremities, shock, delirium and kidney failure.
Treatment: Antibiotics
Avoidance: Avoid mosquitoes; wear protective clothing and insect repellant.

Tasting the Black Vomit

Epidemics were quite common in early Texas. During the 19th century, Texans battled several outbreaks of cholera, small pox, measles, dengue fever, diphtheria and whooping cough. One of the more frightening epidemic diseases was Yellow Fever, which burned through the Galveston area no less than nine times between 1839 and 1867. Yellow Fever was especially frightening given the quick onslaught of illness and suffering. People who seemed perfectly healthy would often die within three days of becoming infected. During the short course of the illness, infected persons suffered fevers, pain and uncontrollable vomiting of blood clots (called black vomit).

Now known to be carried by infected mosquitoes, contracting Yellow Fever at the time was suspect to any number of theories. Some believed the disease was the result of air particles emanating from garbage or stagnant water. Others believed it was transmitted through human-to-human contact. In an effort to disprove the later theory and put an end to the extremely poor living conditions of quarantine camps, Ashbel Smith tasted the black vomit from several different patients during the epidemic of 1839. Despite his failure to contract Yellow Fever after his "taste test," Galvestonians continued to isolate those with the disease as well as quarantine incoming ships.

It wasn't until much later that the true source of the disease was discovered.

INSECTS, ARACHNIDS, WORMS AND PARASITES

We retraced our steps to a clear spring, near the house, and despite the mosquitoes,—which abounded in the thousand— camped for the night.

— W. B. Parker, 1854

It is estimated that between 25,000 and 30,000 species and subspecies of insects make their home in Texas. Just as with other forms of fauna and flora, some of these species are not native to Texas; the most famous of these uninvited guests are the fire ant and Africanized or so-called Killer Bees. Although contact with insects and arachnids while afield (or even indoors) is realistically unavoidable, commercial insect repellants and other precautionary methods can minimize discomfort and annoyance. And in some extreme cases an unexpected trip to the hospital or morgue.

ANTS

Fire ant
Solenopsis invicta Buren

Of the more than 210 species of ants inhabiting Texas, the fire ant or Texas red imported fire ant is the most destructive and likely to disturb hunters. Each year fire ants cost the state of Texas an estimated $1.2 billion in damage and control efforts.

Originally from South America, fire ants first entered the United States in soil or plant matter via cargo vessels docking in Mobile, Alabama, in the early 1930s. The ant's extremely aggressive nature helped them to spread quickly, and it is believed that they entered Texas in the 1950s. Since that time they have spread throughout the majority of the state, thriving in almost every type of environment.

They are a medium-sized ant and can easily be located by their large mounds of loose soil that average upwards of 18 inches in diameter. These mounds can be destroyed with a variety of pesticides although several applications may be necessary.

Triggered by vibration and movement, fire ants will sting whatever they happen to be on once it moves. In the case of humans or animals, this can lead to a painful encounter, especially when considering that fire ants

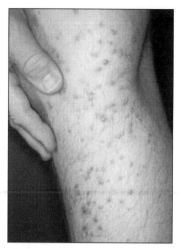

Getting into a swarm of fire ants can ruin any hunter's day.

often swarm. These swarms are capable of killing songbirds, smaller mammals and reptiles and even whitetail fawns.

Their sting is not lethal, however, and a very small percentage of the population may experience a severe allergic reaction. Persons who experience reactions should seek medical attention immediately.

Treatment: Anesthetic cream.

Centipedes and Millipedes

Not insects, but rather the distant relatives of lobsters and crawfish, centipedes and millipedes prefer moist habitats with high humidity. Although somewhat similar in appearance, centipedes have only one pair of legs per body segment while millipedes have two pair per segment. Centipedes also tend to be flatter where millipedes have a more rounded body. Neither creature is a great threat to humans.

When bothered, however, a centipede can deliver a painful bite with a fair amount of poison behind it. This is especially true of some of the larger species in the state, some of which reach a length of 6 or more inches. Despite the pain involved, the bite is relatively harmless unless the person is allergic to the poison.

Millipedes do not bite but will produce an irritating or smelly fluid from their repugnatorial glands. This fluid—aside from sometimes smelling bad—is harmless unless a person is allergic.

Millipede

Treatment: Persons who come in contact with millipede fluid should clean the area thoroughly with soap and water. Treat a bite with an ice pack. Persons who experience an allergic reaction should seek medical attention immediately.

Chigger

Also referred to as jiggers and redbugs, chiggers are one of the most despised pests in Texas. Closely related to ticks and spiders, chiggers feed on snakes, turtles, mammals, birds and humans. Chiggers are so small that most people are only able to see them with the aid of a magnifying glass. These 1/20 to 1/64-inch parasites are orange to yellow to bright red with hairy bodies. In the larval stage, they have three pair of legs. In the nymph and adult stage, they have four pair.

Chiggers are only parasitic in the larval stage. Contrary to popular opinion, chiggers do not suck blood or burrow into the skin. Rather, they pierce the skin to inject a salivary secretion of digestive enzymes that break down skin cells. The liquefied result is sucked up as food. This process causes an itchy red welt on the skin.

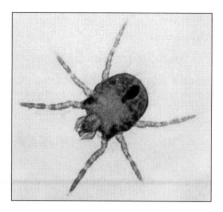

As with any pest, precaution and repellant are the best path to avoidance. If exposure does occur, a hot bath or shower will most likely kill the still-attached larva. However, the infected skin will most likely itch for up to five days.

Treatment: Anesthetic cream.

Fleas

Fleas are extremely small, wingless insects that feed on the blood of animals and humans. Of all the species of fleas in Texas, the cat flea (*Ctenocephalides felis*) is the most common and most likely to cause problems for hunters. Found on raccoons, coyotes, pigs, deer and various other animals, fleas can easily jump onto hunters if precautions aren't made. The best of these is to wear insecticide when afield and to always wear long clothing as well as rubber gloves when skinning animals.

Treatment: Anesthetic or topical steroid creams, calamine-containing lotions, oral antihistamines.

Leeches

Although most of the leeches found in Texas are relatively small, the two species that are most likely to cause trouble for humans (*Macrobdella decora* and *Philobdella gracilis*) are capable of reaching up to 6 inches in length. Just like their smaller kin, these large worm-like creatures have a well-developed sucker at the tail end of their body and a lesser-developed one around the mouth. The suckers are used to drink blood through a host's skin.

Leeches are found in most bodies of water and spend most of their time attached to turtles, fish and frogs. Leeches do not transmit human diseases and the damage they do to skin is minimal. Attached leeches can be removed by hand, with table salt or with a fire source although the latter isn't recommended.

Treatment: Clean the area with soap and water or rubbing alcohol. Antiseptic cream can relieve irritation.

Mosquitoes

The mosquitoes are so big along the Gulf Coast that the inhabitants use mousetraps to catch them.

— Texas saying

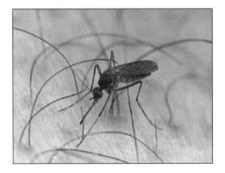

In addition to producing painful and itchy welts, mosquitoes are responsible for transmitting some of the deadliest diseases in Texas history. Yellow fever, malaria, West Nile virus, as well as a host of other potentially deadly diseases have all been spread by some of the more than 80 species of mosquitoes found in Texas.

Commercial repellants (especially those containing DEET), long clothing, head nets and mosquito netting offer the best protection against being bit while afield.

Treatment: Antiseptic cream.

Puss or Asp Caterpillar
Megalopyge opercularis

Deriving its name from the long, Persian cat-like hair covering it in the larva or caterpillar stage, the puss caterpillar is the most poisonous caterpillar in Texas. The threat comes from the venomous spines  contained within the fur. When these spines meet human skin, they cause an extremely painful, burning like sensation. Further reaction to the venom includes numbness, tingling, rashes and blisters. In rare cases, chest pain and anaphylaxis occur.

Puss caterpillars vary from grayish-white to brown to charcoal. A bright orange streak or line often runs the length of the larva. The moth stage, often called a Southern moth or puss moth, is not poisonous.

Treatment: Ice packs and antiseptic cream.

Scorpions

All of the 18 species of scorpions in Texas are capable of producing a painful sting that may produce an allergic reaction. Although none of these species are considered deadly, it is best to watch those that have been bitten for signs of reaction.

Scorpions in Texas are relatively small, most averaging between 2 and 3 inches in length. They are found throughout the state in a variety of habitats although most are found under rocks, rotten logs and other tight spaces where they wait or search for prey. Some species dig burrows in soil. Scorpions are also fond of climbing into dark areas such as boots or wadded clothing.

Treatment: Rinse sting with ammonia. Use antiseptic cream for burning or itching.

SPIDERS

Of the 900 or so species of spiders in Texas, nine pose a real threat to humans: the four species of widow spiders and five species of recluse spider. Other species, such as tarantulas, are large enough to inflect a painful bite but are not poisonous.

Recluse Spiders

Apache recluse *(Loxosceles apachae)*
Big Bend recluse *(Loxosceles blanda)*
Brown recluse *(Loxosceles recluse)*
Mediterranean recluse *(Loxosceles rufescens)*
Texas recluse *(Loxosceles devia)*

Of the five species of recluse spider known to Texas only the brown and Mediterranean (a non-native species) are known to be venomous to humans. Regardless, the remaining three should still be avoided due to the potential danger of an allergic reaction.

Like most spiders, the brown and Mediterranean recluse spiders are most often found in tight, confined spaces such as under rocks, logs, branches and limbs. Closer to home, or camp, they are found in bathrooms, under furniture, behind baseboards, and in wadded clothing and shoes. Recluse spiders are nocturnal, spending the night hunting a variety of insects and other arthropods. With legs fully extended these species of spider are roughly the size of a half dollar. They vary from orange to yellow to dark brown. Unlike most other species of spider, recluses have only six eyes. These are separated into three pairs and arranged in a semicircle pattern on the head that forms the base of a violin-like mark along the back.

The bite of these spiders may be intense or only fairly noticeable. The effect may be immediate or delayed from between 24 to 36 hours. Symptoms may include intense pain at the site of the bite, fever, chills, nausea, weakness, joint pain and restlessness.

Treatment: Seek medical attention.

Widow Spiders

Brown widow *(Latrodectus geometricus)*
Northern black widow *(Latrodectus various)*
Southern black widow *(Latrodectus mactans)*
Western black widow *(Latrodectus hesperus)*

Found in protected cavities, under rocks and limbs, or on the undersides of plants, members of the widow species are naturally shy and retiring. They are typically black but different colorations are quite common. All are marked with two red triangles on the underside of the abdomen that more often than not form an hourglass shape. Some

The Black Widow Spider

males and juveniles exhibit orange, white or red markings on their back. Average adult size is about one inch in length.

Widow spiders are so named because in some species, the female eats the male after mating, thus leaving the female a widow. Widow spiders are not named for producing widows in the human species due to their poisonous bite. In fact, less than 5 percent of the people bitten by widow spiders die.

The bite of a widow spider is so minute that most people fail to feel it. However, the aftereffects of the bite are generally felt within three hours. Symptoms include tremors, nausea, vomiting, leg cramps, abdominal pain, profuse perspiration, loss of muscle tone and a rise in blood pressure. Some individuals also experience breathing difficulties or fall unconscious. The bit area is only slightly noticeable, exhibiting two small puncture wounds and mild swelling.

Treatment: Seek medical attention.

Stinging insects

Bees (Africanized, European, etc.) and wasps (yellow jackets, mud daubers, hornets, etc.) can be found almost anywhere in Texas. Some species, such as yellow jackets and paper wasps, are especially fond of building nests in deer stands and in and around camps. Likewise, bees will establish a colony in any isolated, dry area.

As with any insects that can potentially cause harm, avoidance is the best plan of action.

Treatment: Scrape stinger free from skin if still attached. Do not use tweezers or squeeze stinger, as this will most likely inject more venom. Apply ice packs or meat tenderizer to stung area to assuage pain. Seek medical attention immediately if severely allergic.

Ticks

The estimated 30 to 35 species of ticks in Texas carry a multitude of diseases, including Lyme disease, Rocky Mountain Spotted Fever, Ehrlichiosis and relapsing fever. Ticks are found throughout the state in almost every type of environment although there are fewer species found in the western portion of the state.

The best way to avoid encounters with ticks is by using commercial insect repellent, by tucking pants into boots or socks so ticks do not have access to skin and by wearing light colored clothing so ticks can easily be seen.

Treatment: Use tweezers to remove a tick by grabbing it as close to the skin as possible. Do not squeeze a tick or touch it with bare hands. Check skin for any remaining tick parts. Clean the area with soap and water. Make a note of the date in case of further medical problems.

Worms

Usually found in contaminated food or water, parasitic worms such as pinworms, hookworms, whipworms and roundworms cause infection and spread diseases throughout the world. It is estimated that more than 500 million people worldwide are infected with pinworm alone. Fortunately, parasitic worms are easily avoidable.

- Make sure that all food is clean and well prepared.
- Cook all meat thoroughly.
- Do not drink untreated water.
- Maintain proper hygiene.
- Always wear latex gloves when cleaning game.

REPTILES

Texas ranks first in the number of reptilian species in the United States. Thirty-five species of turtles, 61 of lizards, 68 of snake, and one crocodilian all make their home in the Lone Star State. Fortunately, most of these are fairly harmless and go out of their way to avoid human contact.

Alligators, although the largest and most dangerous predator in the state, are naturally shy and reclusive. So much in fact that it could easily be successfully argued that the landscape they inhabit offers more potential danger than the animal itself.

The fact that the snapping turtle and alligator snapping turtle can easily severe a finger from a hand doesn't necessarily make it dangerous. Those that have discovered this power firsthand (no pun intended) were most likely not charged by the animal.

Although some of the lizards within the state are covered in "horns," none are dangerous or poisonous. Some feel that the more horns that cover a lizard the better, as is the case with the Texas horned lizard, or horny toad, which is the official state lizard.

The only reptile that poses any real threat, and only when confronted or disturbed, are the 15 species of poisonous snakes (out of 68 snake species in the state). And even still, the odds of getting struck by lightning are far greater than getting bit by a poisonous snake. The best way to beat the odds is by giving all snakes room.

Copperhead

Southern copperhead *(Agkistrodon contortrix contorix)*
Broad-banded copperhead *(Agkistrodon contortrix laticinctus)*
Trans-Pecos copperhead *(Agkistrodon contortrix pictigaster)*

Kill a copperhead and its mate will seek revenge.
— Texas folk saying

There are three species of copperhead snakes in Texas: the Southern copperhead, found in east Texas; the broad-banded copperhead, found in the central portion of the state; and the Trans-Pecos copperhead, found in the Big Bend area. All are similar in coloring, size and habits.

Averaging between 18 and 38 inches in length, copperheads are tan to fawn with vertical brown to copper colored bands. Eyes are copper colored. They eat a variety of prey, including insects, frogs, small rodents and birds. Copperheads have easily adapted to life near man but because of their camouflage and fairly gentle disposition, they are seldom seen.

In terms of potency, copperhead venom is not especially threatening if medical treatment is immediately sought. During a 10-year study in Texas of copperhead venom's toxicity, not a single person died of the 308 on record as having been bitten.

Coral Snake
Micrurus fulvius tenere

> *From its beautiful colors and harmless appearance it is likely to*
> *be handled carelessly, and its bite is dangerous.*
> — *Biological Survey of Texas, 1889-1905*

One would be hard pressed to find an individual in rural Texas that couldn't make the distinction between the poisonous coral snake and the harmless milk or scarlet snakes by reciting "Red n' yellow kill a fellow, Red n' black venom lack" or a variation thereof. This colloquial saying deals with all coral snakes. The coral snake's skin is a brightly colored series of black, red and yellow cross bands. The yellow and red bands touching one another remind all that it is poisonous. Although made up of the same colors, the yellow and red bands on the milk and scarlet snake do not touch.

The bright colors on the coral snake don't necessarily act as a warning of its poisonous nature but rather is believed to be camouflage. These colors appear quite different during the evening hours when the snake is most active.

Coral snakes average between 24 and 26 inches in length with males generally being shorter. It is interesting to note that although these measurements are the average, the longest coral snake on record was almost twice this, measuring 47 inches.

Coral snakes are quite common and are found throughout the majority of south, central and east Texas. They prefer heavy cover but are perfectly at home in the manicured gardens and hedgerows of suburbia as well. Nocturnal by nature, Coral snakes generally eat other snakes but are known to eat skinks and lizards as well.

The venom of the coral snake is extremely toxic and powerful. It is eight times more lethal than that of the western diamondback and equal in potency to a cobra's. Still, the coral snake's shy demeanor and small peg-like fangs make it one of the least dangerous of the poisonous snakes in Texas.

Rattlesnakes

Banded rock rattlesnake *(Crotalus lepidus klauberi)*

Desert massasauga*(Sistrurus catenatus edwardsii)*

Mojave rattlesnake *(Crotalus scutulatus scutulatus)*

Mottled rock rattlesnake *(Crotalus lepidus lepidus)*

Northern blacktail rattlesnake *(Crotalus molossus molossus)*

Prairie rattlesnake *(Crotalus viridis viridis)*

Timber rattlesnake *(Crotalus horridus)*

Western diamondback rattlesnake *(Crotalus atrox)*

Western massasauga *(Sistrurus catenatus tergeminus)*

Western pigmy rattlesnake *(Sistrurus miliarius streckeri)*

A bright moon shone over us on this our last march before reaching the Upper Cross Timbers. In fine spirits our party rolled along, cracking jokes and caroling snatches of wild song, when just as we passed the brow of a hill, our harmony was checked by a rapid k-r-r-r-r k-r-r-r-r, rattle, rattle, rattle, and a voice exclaimed, "look out, look to your left," and sure enough, there, almost under my horse's feet and coiled ready to strike, lay an enormous diamond rattlesnake, looking ten times more deadly in the moonlight. Bang! Bang! went revolvers—k-r-r-r-r, k-r-r-r-r, went the rattle—"there he goes,"—"here he is,"—"there, hit him with your ramrod,"—"ah, that will do,"—"now bring him out."...—and there he hung, six-feet long and eleven rattles.

— W. B. Parker, 1854

Only Arizona has more species of rattlesnake than does Texas. Despite coming in second, Texas still has more than enough species and subspecies of rattlers to blanket every vegetational zone in the state. Ten species and subspecies of rattlesnake make their home in Texas. Of these, only three have any significant interaction with humans: the western diamondback, the prairie and the eastern timber or canebreak.

Perhaps the most vilified creature in the mythic West of pulp fiction and Western cinema, the western diamondback is the largest and most widespread poisonous snake in Texas. It is found in almost every region of the state except the northeastern corner of the Panhandle and the extreme east Pineywoods. It averages between three and four feet in length but is capable of reaching upwards of seven and one-half feet. Although many argue diamondbacks can reach lengths much greater than this, proof of such specimens is nonexistent. Skins that offer evidence of larger specimens have often been stretched as much as 25 percent in length.

Western diamondback rattler.

A diamondback's coloration varies due to environment but most are brown to tan with diamond-shaped vertebral blotches. The tail is clearly marked with alternating black and white stripes. Like all rattlesnakes, the diamondback grows a new rattle segment with each skin shedding. As these rattles grow brittle and often break off, they do not give an accurate indication of age.

Western diamondbacks prey mainly on birds, small mammals and rabbits.

Due to its widespread distribution and fairly aggressive temperament, diamondbacks account for the majority of snakebites in Texas. Despite the snake's extremely toxic venom, advances in treatment have kept the fatality rate of those bitten to less than 10 percent.

Although smaller than the western diamondback, averaging between two and four and one-half feet in length, the prairie rattlesnake is no less dangerous. Actually it is more so, having slightly more lethal venom. Found throughout the Panhandle and Trans-Pecos sections of the state, Prairie rattlesnakes are tan to brown with between 35 and 55 oval-shaped brown patches covering the back. The tail is banded with tan and brown stripes. Prey includes lizards, small mammals and birds.

Often called a canebreaker or a canebreak rattler, the timber rattlesnake is found throughout the eastern third of the state. It averages between 2 and 5-feet in length. It is dark brown to tan with dark brown chevrons and rust colored stripes along the back. The tail is solid black. Its prey is mainly small mammals and birds.

There are two rock rattlesnakes in Texas: the mottled rock rattlesnake and the banded rock rattlesnake. Both are highly prized by collectors because of their unique coloration and as a result, they are protected by law. Both are relatively small snakes, averaging less than two feet in length and both prey on lizards, mice and amphibians. The more common of the two rock rattlers is the mottled.

Coloration of the mottled rattlesnake varies depending upon where it lives in the southwestern quarter of the state but is generally pinkish to gray with either black or soft gray dorsal stripes.

Found in only two westernmost counties in Texas, the banded rock rattlesnake is silvery white with black cross bands.

The desert massasauga averages less than two feet in length and is found in the western third of the state as well as the extreme south. It is grayish white with brown dorsal splotches. Prey includes lizards, mice, snakes and frogs.

Similar in size, color and diet is the western massasauga. It is found in a wide band running between the eastern sections of the Panhandle to the eastern Gulf Coast.

The Mojave rattlesnake is found in the western portion of the state, from the Big Bend region to the western border. It averages between two and four feet in length. It resembles the western diamondback in coloration but is much more aggressive. It preys on mice.

The northern blacktail rattlesnake inhabits the same area as the Mojave but extends its range farther east. It is similar in markings although much darker. Size and prey are also similar.

As the name implies, the Western pigmy rattlesnake is fairly small, averaging between 14 and 20 inches in length. Despite having the western moniker it is found in the extreme eastern section of the state. It is grayish pink with small black circular markings along the back. It preys on small reptiles, amphibians and insects.

Western cottonmouth
Agkistrodon piscivorus leucostoma

The western cottonmouth or water moccasin is the subject of one of the most persistent urban (or rural) myths in Texas. As the story goes, a water skier on a Texas lake fell into a nest of cottonmouths and was immediately killed as the result of hundreds if not thousands of snakebites. Despite there being absolutely no proof that this event ever took place,

the story has only helped in fueling the cottonmouth's already exaggerated reputation for tenacious behavior. Although cottonmouths can be aggressive, especially when confronted, only 7 percent of those bitten by poisonous snakes are the result of an encounter with a cottonmouth.

Averaging between two and five feet in length, cottonmouths are dark brown to olive green to black. They are found throughout the central and eastern portion of the state in varying types of environment although semi-aquatic areas are preferred. Prey includes fish, frogs, water snakes and mammals as large as muskrats.

Cottonmouths are excellent swimmers and unlike other water snakes that constantly wriggle when swimming, cottonmouths frequently stop and float on the surface. It is during this float time when fishermen most often surprise them. During such encounters, cottonmouths gape openmouthed in threat and warning, displaying the white mouth that gives them their name.

Snake Bite Treatment
- Get the victim to the nearest medical personnel immediately.
- Try to keep victim calm to slow the spread of venom.
- Do not cut wound, apply a tourniquet, attempt to suck out the poison or give the victim caffeinated or alcoholic beverages.

Snakes for Cash

Joey Burleson was never one to let an opportunity get away, even if the opportunity was six feet of angry rattlesnake.

Growing up on a ranch in the harsh and desolate scrubland of South Texas with the nearest town a hard drive of 25 miles away, Joey made the most of his surroundings. All his life, he's worked on his family's ranch, guided hunters and worked for a local surveyor. But four years ago, at age 14, he discovered that the easiest money was lying on the ground all around him, just waiting to be picked up. That's when he discovered rattlesnakes.

Joey finds rattlers almost everywhere: on the property he works, around his house and sunning on *senderos* and highways.

"Sometimes I can get five or six on the way to school if they don't put up too big of a fight."

The live snakes are sold to taxidermists, hunters, labs for venom and to a guy that "buys them for their meat and skin" for upwards of $40 per snake. Joey has gotten so good at his trade that he often uses nothing more than his bare hands to wrangle the serpents.

When asked if his high school principal minds his having a truck bed full of live snakes in the parking lot, Joey grinningly replies, "Don't know. I never asked him."

—*This article first appeared in* Outdoor Life

6

CLOTHING & EQUIPMENT

Hunting actually requires very little in the way of equipment. In addition to a place to hunt, all that is needed is the hunter's weapon of choice. Despite this simplicity hunters are notorious for wanting to own the latest and greatest equipment. In 2004 alone, the last year for which statistics are available, hunters in the United States spent nearly $3 billon on hunting related clothing and equipment.

While there's a good chance that a great number of these purchases were probably impulsive or frivolous, the right clothing and equipment can not only improve a hunter's chances at taking game but can also keep hunters safe and prepared for any emergency. The following list was compiled with all three of these criteria in mind.

CLOTHING

> *"While hunting I wore heavy shoes, with hobnails or rubber soles; khaki trousers, the knees faced with leather, and the legs buttoning tight from the knee to below the ankle, to avoid the need of leggings; a khaki-colored army shirt; and sun helmet, which I wore in deference to local advice, instead of my beloved and far more convenient slouch hat."*
> — Theodore Roosevelt, *African Game Trails*

Brush Country *owner Paul Harris with a beautiful East Texas buck.*

Hunting opportunities occur throughout the year in Texas. Although deer season takes place in the winter, hogs, predators, some small game and exotics can be hunted year-round. Because of this, and due to the extreme nature of Texas weather, appropriate hunting attire varies greatly. Still, hunting clothing in Texas falls into two major categories: camouflage and safari.

Sometimes in Texas it seems as though everyone wears camo. Hunters wear it bow hunting, rifle hunting, to the mall, around the house and around town. In some circles, camo wear is nothing more than casual wear. Outside of clothing, camo appears on trucks, SUVs, golf carts, blinds, linens, furniture and home décor. Even Teddy bears and lingerie have failed to escape the trend to conceal everything in a greenish pattern.

Camo clothing comes in countless patterns and in a multitude of styles. Because of the varying landscape and vegetation, no one pattern works everywhere in the state. However, some Texas-based companies have come close.

Founded in Bryan, *Brush Country's* camouflage pattern is an eight-colored palette of mesquite, thorns, cactus and live oak with remarkable 3-D realism. Despite its vegetational makeup, the pattern works well throughout the state. *Brush Country* camo is especially popular with predator and archery hunters who swear by the pattern's ability to allow them to "disappear" in the wild. *Brush Country* also manufactures a line of clothing in association with the *Texas Trophy Hunters Association.*

Located in Laredo, *Bushlan* camouflage manufactures two different colored patterns to blend into the natural state of Texas. *Bushlan's Classic Green* is designed for use in coastal forests and brush country while the company's *Classic Brown* is for semi-arid high desert and brush. Both patterns work extremely well and are popular with hunters and non-hunters throughout the state.

Bushlan Camo

Often worn on game ranches, as well as afield, traditional safari wear is also quite popular in Texas. Born out of more than a century of trial and error on the Dark Continent, traditional safari clothing is just as utilitarian and fashionable in the Lone Star State. Several Texas-based companies either carry or import safari clothing for Texas hunters.

Established in Zimbabwe in 1990, but headquartered in Houston, *TAG Safari* carries hunting attire the likes of which have even been seen on former President (and honorary Texan) George Bush. Their clothing is pigment dyed to match specific topography. *TAG Safari's*

Gander Mountain *safari clothing*

Vice President Jin Laxmidas explains, "Khaki has always been the favorite of safari travelers, since the sandy tan color does not show any dust. Stone is a favorite of those who like to hunt the deserts. Olive is an all-time favorite and suited to the muddy river shores and to long adventures away from the camp, when laundry is available after long intervals."

Also headquartered in Houston is *Texas Safari Hunting Products*. Although primarily known for their first product, the *Texas Safari Rifle Vest*, *TSHP* manufactures a number of shirts, t-shirts and caps.

Other manufacturers of safari clothing include *Cabela's, Gander Mountain*, and *Long Grass Outfitters* (another Texas-based company).

Catering exclusively to female hunters, *She Safari* of Conroe manufactures a variety of clothing in both traditional safari wear and camouflage. Unlike some manufacturers that simply alter their clothing designs to fit women, *She Safari's* clothing is specifically designed for women. With the ever-growing number of female hunters, companies such as this are long overdue.

Regardless of the style of clothing chosen, materials and construction should be durable for the harsh conditions of the outdoors. Likewise, clothing should be comfortable and well fitted.

Hunters should prepare for dramatic weather changes when afield and dress

Pam Zaitz of She Safari

accordingly. Dressing in layers is often the best way to handle the possibility of extreme weather, since clothing can be removed or added as needed.

Below is a checklist of suggested clothing for hunting in Texas. Of course, not all items are applicable to every situation.

NOTE: Safety orange is not required on private land but is required on public land while hunting with rifle or shotgun. Hunters should keep this in mind when planning their attire.

Underwear
Regular or long, depending upon weather and preference.

Pants
Pants should be comfortable as well as durable. Pants that convert to shorts are great in warmer months (of course in Texas that could be any month). Large rubber bands can help cinch pant legs tight, in turn keeping out insects and debris.

Shirt
Whether button-up or pullover, collared or collarless, shirts should be able to withstand the elements. Long sleeve shirts with buttons that allow sleeves to be rolled up and held in place can make adapting to the temperature easier.

Vest
Safari style or down filled, depending on the season and temperature, are recommended.

Windbreaker
Light models that roll into their own storage bag are easy to carry and always ready.

Jacket
Whether made of synthetic or natural fibers, comfort and warmth should be the first consideration.

Overalls

Overalls and bib suits that fit over normal clothing and offer a wealth of heat are perfect for freezing temperatures or for sitting motionless for a time.

Scarf, Bandana, Shemagh and Balaclavas

These items offer protection for the face and neck during inclement weather. Growing in popularity, the shemagh can also be worn around the head for extra warmth. Balaclavas adapt to several different positions, from neck wrap to head covering.

Parka/Rain Gear

They should be lightweight and always nearby. In an emergency, a parka can be used as a ground cloth or as a roof in a protective structure.

Belt

Belts should be strong enough to hold knives, ammunition cartridges and all the other items hunters find to hang from them.

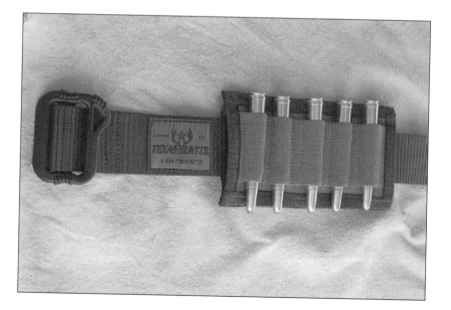

Hat

A hat is used to protect the head from sun, heat, cold or rain. Although camouflage and safari styles are fairly common, by far the most popular choice is the traditional cowboy hat.

Gloves

Gloves will keep hands not only warm, but can also offer protection from cuts, thorns and windburn. Lined leather gloves are also a good choice in fair to cold weather.

Footwear

While cowboy boots are by far the most popular style of boots in Texas, they weren't designed for walking great distances. They were designed for riding horses and dancing the two-step. In addition, cowboy boots have an inadequate sole for most Texas terrain and they lack essential ankle support.

By far the best boots for hunting are those made specifically for the individual hunter. In the Golden Age of Safari, British hunters would have several pairs of custom made hunting boots created for their time afield. Today, finding a custom boot maker can be a little more difficult. One company that still makes boots the old-fashioned way is *Russell Moccasin*. They make boots based on an extensive list of measurements from the hunter's foot so they fit and wear like a second skin. True, custom made boots can be pricey but considering what your feet can go through during a weekend hog hunt, the cost of truly protecting them doesn't seem that outlandish.

Of course, there are plenty of quality boot makers that make boots in standard sizes. *Cabela's* and *Gander Mountain* store brand boots are well made and affordable, as are *Filson, Red Wing* and a host of others.

Regardless of the maker, boots should be comfortable, offer plenty of arch and ankle support, and have a sole applicable to the environment to be hunted (boots best suited for climbing are of little use in the flat pine forests of East Texas).

From left to right, the author's cowboy boots, Cabela's Insulated Woodsman *and* Russell Moccasin Mountain PH—*all well used and seasoned but not all suited for hunting. Be sure to match the boot to the area to be hunted.*

A good choice for the potentially hazardous environment of South and West Texas are snake boots. Not only do snake boots protect hunters from possible serpent encounters, but they also protect feet and legs against thorns and cactus. They also provide a great deal of protection from insects and fairly deep water and are an excellent choice for hunting at night when the ground isn't always visible.

During cooler weather or when hunting in relatively open terrain, traditional or ankle boots are more than adequate. Regardless of the style chosen, boots should be well worn in before taking to the field. Nothing can ruin a hunt faster than uncomfortable feet or feet covered in cuts and blisters.

While most hunters spend a great deal of time and thought in selecting the proper pair of boots, they spend little time on what actually touches their feet: socks. Socks should be comfortable, form fitting and keep feet warm and dry. Some of the best socks on the market are the *Falke* line from *Westley Richards*, which are anatomically formed and padded for the individual left and right foot. Wearing them is similar to having an extra instep in your boot.

Lock it Up

It is unlawful to store, transport or abandon an unsecured firearm in a place where children are likely to be and can obtain access to the firearm.

— *Texas Penal Code*, Section 46.13.

Texas law requires that firearms be kept secure and out of the reach of children. While trigger and cable locks keep weapons from being discharged, these measures don't keep them from being handled. The best place for any firearm is behind lock and key. Today's gun safes not only make this possible but also protect firearms and other valuables from theft, fire and loss. Gun safes are also affordable and come in a variety of styles and configurations.

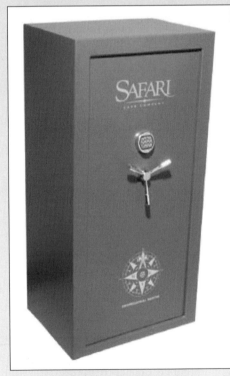

Safari Professional Hunter Series

The best-selling gun safes in the United States are from *Liberty Safe and Security Products, Inc.* Because of their above-industry standards in furnace testing, they are also considered to be among the best made. In addition to their own safe line, *Liberty* also manufactures the in-store brand of *Gander Mountain* safes.

In addition to offering excellent fire protection, safes from *Cannon* and *Safari* offer a *"no-cost warranty,"* meaning owners are out nothing for repairs if the safe is damaged by theft or attempted forced entry. *Safari* and *Cannon* safes also offer *"Tru Rack."* According to the manufacturers, this rack system actually holds a rifle in each slot, something other safes claim to do but don't always deliver.

Gun owners who want the security of a safe without having their weapons out of view now have the option of doing so thanks to the *GunSafe Company.* This relatively new company manufactures traditional gun cabinets from such top grade woods as red oak and Northern cherry. Hidden within the wooden crossbars are steel bars, making theft almost impossible. The only way to remove firearms without a key would be to destroy the cabinet.

Traveling with a firearm? Try placing your rifle inside a soft case before securing it inside a hard case. This not only offers double protection but also allows you to have an easier way to carry around your firearm once you reach your destination. TZ Case *metal hard case and* Texas Hunt Company *universal gun case pictured.*

When traveling, the best way to secure a firearm is with a locked hard case. Metal cases that are airline approved seem able to take the most punishment. *TZ Case, Cabela's* and *Gander Mountain* all make quality metal gun cases.

EQUIPMENT

Optics

Quality optics are essential to hunting in Texas. Whether in the thick forests of the Pineywoods region or in the extreme openness of West Texas, proper optics help locate and identify trophy game. Of course not all optics are suited to all sections of the state. Spotting scopes are relatively useless in the thick woods of East Texas, likewise are compact binoculars on an aoudad hunt in the Davis Mountains. For this reason, it is important to match the type of optic used and the magnification available to the area being hunted. A general rule of thumb to follow is the bigger the country, the bigger the optics should be.

Binoculars and spotting scopes should be of the best affordable quality and allow for the most light transmission. With recent technological advances in design and production, companies such as *Meopta* are able to produce binoculars and spotting scopes with upwards of 99.8 percent light transmission. This is extremely beneficial when

Good binoculars are a must when hunting in Texas.
On the left is an old pair of Leitz *that served the author's grandfather well.*
On the right are the author's Meoptas.

hunting the early morning or late evening and in other low light situations. Other manufacturers of superb optics include *Nikon, Steiner, Leica, Swarovski, Zeiss, Bushnell* and *Leupold.*

Other important features in optics include fully multicoated lenses, a nitrogen purged and sealed body, a comfortable feel and proper eye relief. Weight is also a consideration. These same features also apply to riflescopes.

Further riflescope considerations are reticule size, durability, body size, adjustability and mounting system. Lit or illuminated reticules, such as those available from *Meopta* and *Burris*, are great when hunting in low light or hunting darker colored animals such as javelina and hog.

Completely different from any other riflescope on the market today is the *Digital Hunter* from *Elcan*. The *Digital Hunter* is a fully digital riflescope. This allows for electronic features such as video and still photography, four different reticules including one that allows for ballistic compensation and a powerful zoom. *Eclan* also makes the *Digital Hunter* in a *Day / Night* model with night vision that allows hunters to shoot in complete darkness.

In Texas, certain game animals as well as exotics can be legally hunted at night. Recent advancements and increased market competition have brought high quality night vision and night vision riflescopes to semi-affordable prices. Night vision products have changed considerably since the technology's introduction during World War II. Today the so-called *Third Generation*, or highest quality, products can literally turn night into day.

Rangefinders have also improved tremendously in the last few years. Today they are relatively inexpensive and extremely accurate, even at great distances. Some are accurate at distances as far as 1,100 yards to within plus or minus three feet. This type of accuracy comes in a wide variety of styles and models. Although most offer little if any magnification, companies such as *Leica* produce combination rangefinder-binoculars. Another popular combination product is the rangefinder-riflescopes offered by *Nikon, Swarovski* and *Zeiss.*

Ear and Eye Protection

Unfortunately, many longtime hunters have had their hearing suffer as a result of many years of hunting without ear protection. With today's knowledge and technology there is no excuse for this type of loss. Earplugs and hearing muffs protect ears from muzzle blasts. Improving upon other hearing protection devices are products such as those from *Walker's Game Ear*.

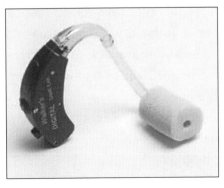

Products such as the *Game Ear I, Game Ear II and Digital Game Ear* (pictured) offer full-blown protection from loud noise but also offer the extra benefit of enhanced hearing. This allows for hunters to hear even the faintest of sounds when afield. Additionally, products such as these allow for hunters to carry on a conversation in normal tones. Basic ear protection doesn't. Other manufactures of ear protection include *Sport Ear* and *Pro Ears*.

Eye protection is a necessity when hunting, especially when doing so in thick scrub where branches and twigs can easily snap or swing into eyes. Eye protection is also safety insurance against weapons malfunctions, blowbacks and flying debris.

Knives

Knives have been used in Texas for everything from skinning and gutting game, eating a meal, opening a bottle or can, killing alligators or hogs to defending the Alamo. Much like with firearms, knife choice is a matter of personal preference. Volumes of books have been written on knife selection and usage as well as on knives that qualify as high art. Regardless of choice or intended usage, a proper knife should be of quality design and construction, comfortable to the user, and above all, sharp.

For pure utilitarian usage in the field it is hard to beat the *Revolver* (pictured) from *Sog Knives*. This model offers a 5-inch blade with "gut hook" as well as a 5-inch bone saw. Access to each blade is made by simply "revolving" the unwanted blade back into the handle.

GPS, Compass, Maps

With the widespread availability of hand-held Global Positioning Systems, or GPS, and updated satellite topographical maps, finding the best place to hunt on a set piece of land has never been easier. GPS units can offer hunter's the location, elevation and the easiest route to a specific location. GPS units are extremely helpful when hunting on unfamiliar public land or when mapping out stand locations on deer leases or private land. More advanced models such as those from *Garmin* and *Magellan* allow hunters to download maps and transfer information to a computer.

No matter how advanced GPS units are, they are of no benefit when their batteries are dead. Hunters should never go afield without a compass and the knowledge of how to use it.

Flashlight

Prime time for hunting most game is just after sunup and just before sundown. Regardless of which part of the day hunters choose to hunt, chances are at some time during the outing they'll be in the dark. Because of this, dependable, quality flashlights are a must.

In the past few years, most flashlight manufacturers have embraced the usage of LED lights. These tiny bulbs are rated as three to four times as bright as conventional flashlight bulbs, produce almost no heat and never burn out. Perhaps the best maker of LED flashlights was one of the first to embrace this technology. Although a bit on the pricy side, *Surefire* flashlights are well worth the investment. They are extremely dependable and their machined-aluminum bodies have been known to deflect a bullet in combat situations. The company's smaller *Executive* series is perfect for small tasks such as going to and from a blind in the dark, reading a map or going to the bathroom in an unfamiliar camp. The *Executive* series can perform double duty when colored filters are utilized. A blue filter helps to illuminate blood while a red filter is invisible to animals, making getting around in the dark without spooking game all the easier. These same features can also be found on the *Legacy Series Illumination Tools* from *Blackhawk*.

For hands-free flashlight usage many hunters rely on headlamps. By wearing a headlamp, hunters can leave both hands free to enter a blind before dark, skin game at night or simply find their way to the bathroom in a dark cabin. *Gander Mountain, Browning, Cabela's, Blackhawk* and *Streamlight* all make dependable and quality headlamps.

Game Cameras

Game cameras are one of the most overlooked tools in hunting. A quality game camera can assist hunters in tracking game movement, locating the best place for a blind and finding trophy game. They can even act as a security system by taking pictures of who comes and goes to camp or a lodge.

Depending on the model, game cameras can utilize standard film or digital images. Some can even capture video. Regardless, all act on the same principal. By utilizing some type of motion sensor, the camera is "tripped" when something moves in front of it.

The best cameras seem to be those that use an invisible infrared flash rather than a conventional flash. This technology allows for crisp, clear pictures in almost total darkness without spooking game. Models such as those from *Leaf River Outdoor Products* allow hunters to review captured digital images with a small monitor on back of the unit or by plugging the unit into a TV or computer. *Moultree Feeders, Cuddleback, Stealthcam* and *Bushnell* also manufacture game cameras.

This buck was caught at night with a Leaf River *game camera.*

Ice Chests

In addition to keeping food and drink cold while afield, ice chests are crucial for transporting game meat and trophies. If there is one consistency in Texas weather it's heat. And ice chests have to be of the utmost quality to handle it.

Despite advances in electric coolers that run on power from a vehicle cigarette lighter, the best coolers are still the standard plastic boxes with plenty of insulation.

7

WHERE TO HUNT

Texas Parks and Wildlife manages hundreds of thousands of acres for public hunting. Access to this land is made available through lottery type drawings or by onsite registration. Information about these two types of hunting is detailed in two separate publications: *Applications for Drawings on Public Hunting Lands* and the *Public Hunting Lands Map Booklet*. Both booklets are available through Texas Parks and Wildlife headquarters or field offices.

Usually made available in July or August, the booklet *Applications for Drawings on Public Hunting Lands* contains information on the upcoming year's hunts available through Texas Parks and Wildlife. Drawings are held for alligator, deer, feral hog, javelina and exotics. Information on special "Guided Hunts," such as big horn sheep, waterbuck, gemsbok and scimitar-horned Oryx, is also given. Hunts take place on Wildlife Management Areas, State Parks and on private land throughout the state. Odds of getting drawn depend on the number of permits available and on the area and species chosen by the hunter. To further help hunters choose an area, statistics from the previous year's hunt, including hunters' success rates, are included in the booklet as well. Some areas have fairly good odds while some of the more popular areas can leave hunters feeling as if they have a better chance of getting struck by lightning than ever getting drawn.

Hunters that aren't drawn for the hunt of their choice are issued "preference points." This program increases a hunter's chances in subsequent years by giving the hunter an "extra chance" for each year he or she was not drawn.

Another program that helps hunters who fail to get drawn is the "Standby Hunter" program. This program allows hunters to try for a chance at an opening at the location of their choice on the day of the hunt. If a drawn hunter fails to show up or additional hunting spots are made available, all "Standby Hunters" are entered into an onsite drawing.

The other publication detailing public hunting opportunities in Texas is made available only to hunters that purchase an Annual Public Hunting Permit (APH). Once purchased, hunters receive the *Public Hunting Lands Map Booklet*. This booklet lists areas and species available for hunting through onsite registration. Game varies from area to area, as does the legal method of harvest.

STATE WILDLIFE MANAGEMENT AREAS

Although some public hunting occurs in State Parks or in State Natural Areas, most occurs on State Wildlife Management Areas (WMA). The following is a listing of WMAs that generally allow hunting through either drawing or onsite registration. Contact individual WMA or Texas Parks and Wildlife for more information.

Alabama Creek WMA

1805 E. Lufkin
Lufkin, TX 75901
936-639-1879

Species Available: Whitetail deer, feral hog, squirrels and rabbits.
Acreage: 14,561

Alazan Bayou WMA

1805 E. Lufkin
Lufkin, TX 75901
936-639-1879

Species Available: Whitetail deer, feral hog and squirrels.
Acreage: 1,973

Angelina Neches/Dam B WMA

1342 S. Wheeler
Jasper, TX 75951
409-384-6894

Species Available: Whitetail deer, feral hog, squirrels and rabbits.
Acreage: 16,360

Bannister WMA

1342 S. Wheeler
Jasper, TX 75951
409-384-6894

Species Available: Whitetail deer, feral hog, squirrels, rabbits
and furbearers.
Acreage: 28,307

Big Lake Bottom WMA

1670 FM 488
Streetman, TX 75859
903-389-7080

Species Available: Whitetail deer, feral hog and squirrels.
Acreage: 1,794

Black Gap WMA

109 S. Cockrell
Alpine, TX 79830
432-837-3251

Species Available: Mule deer, whitetail deer, javelina, coyotes
and rabbits.
Acreage: 107,878

Caddo Lake State Park and WMA

P.O. Box 226
Karnack, TX 75661
903-679-9817

Species Available: Whitetail deer, feral hog, squirrels, rabbits,
predators, furbearers and frogs.
Acreage: 7,681

Caddo National Grasslands WMA

525 Madewell Rd.
Paris, TX 75462
903-982-7107

Species Available: Whitetail deer and squirrels.
Acreage: 16,140

Chaparral WMA

P.O. Box 115
Artesia Wells, TX 78001
830-676-3413

Species Available: Whitetail deer, javelina and rabbits.
Acreage: 15,200

Cooper WMA

829 CR 4795
Suphur Springs, TX 75482-0402
903-945-3132

Species Available: Whitetail deer and feral hog.
Acreage: 14,480

Elephant Mountain WMA

109 S. Cockrell
Alpine, TX 79830
432-837-3251

Species Available: Mule deer, whitetail deer, big horn sheep, free-range elk, javelina and rabbits.
Acreage: 23,147

Gene Howe WMA/ W.A. "Pat" Murphy Unit

15412 FM 2266
Canadian, TX 79014
806-323-8642

Species Available: Rabbit
Acreage: 6,713

Granger WMA

3100 Granger Dam Rd.
Granger, TX 76530
512-859-2668

Species Available: Whitetail deer and feral hog.
Acreage: 11,116

Gus Engeling WMA

16149 North US Hwy 287

Tennessee Colony, TX 75861

903-928-2251

Species Available: Whitetail deer, feral hog and rabbits.

Acreage: 10,958

J.D. Murphree WMA

10 Parks & Wildlife Dr.

Port Arthur, TX 77640

409-736-2551

Species Available: Alligator

Acreage: 24,498

James E. Daughtrey WMA

64 Chaparral WMA Dr.

Cotulla, TX 78014

830-676-3413

Species Available: Whitetail deer, javelina, feral hog and rabbits.

Acreage: 4,400

Keechi Creek WMA

1670 FM 488

Streetman, TX 75859

903-389-7080

Species Available: Whitetail deer, feral hog and squirrel.

Acreage: 1,500

Kerr WMA

2625 FM 1340
Hunt, TX 78024
830-238-4483

Species Available: Whitetail deer, exotics, feral hog and rabbits.
Acreage: 6,493

Las Palomas WMA, Lower Rio Grande Valley Units

154B Lakeview Drive
Weslaco, TX 78596
956-447-2704

Species Available: Whitetail deer, feral hog and rabbits.
Acreage: 5,656

Las Palomas WMA, Ocotillo Unit

109 S. Cockrell
Alpine, TX 79830
432-837-3251

Species Available: Rabbit
Acreage: 2,082

Mad Island WMA

County Courthouse, Room 101
Bay City, TX 77414
979-244-7634

Species Available: Alligator and feral hog.
Acreage: 7,200

Mason Mountain WMA

P.O. Box 1583
Mason, TX 76856
325-347-5037

Species Available: Whitetail deer and exotics.
Acreage: 5,301

Matador WMA

3036 FM 3256
Paducah, TX 79248
806-492-3405

Species Available: Mule deer, whitetail deer and feral hog.
Acreage: 28,183

Matagorda Island WMA

1700 7th St.
Bay City, TX 77414
979-244-6804

Species Available: Whitetail deer and feral hog.
Acreage: 3,900

Moore Plantation WMA

1342 S. Wheeler
Jasper, TX 75951
409-384-6894

Species Available: Whitetail deer, feral hog, furbearers, predators and squirrels.
Acreage: 27,034

North Toledo Bend WMA

1805 E Lufkin
Lufkin, TX 75901
936-639-1879

Species Available: Whitetail deer, feral hog, squirrel and rabbit.
Acreage: 3,650

Old Sabine Bottom WMA

21187 CR 4106
Lindale, TX 75771
903-881-8233

Species Available: Whitetail deer, feral hog, squirrel and rabbit.
Acreage: 5,158

Pat Mayse WMA

525 Madewell Rd
Paris, TX 75462
903-982-7107

Species Available: Whitetail deer, feral hog and squirrel.
Acreage: 8,925

Peach Point WMA

County Courthouse, Room 101
Bay City, TX 77414
979-244-6804

Species Available: Whitetail deer and feral hog.
Acreage: 11,190

Ray Roberts Lake WMA

121 CR 3131
Decatur, TX 76234
940-627-5475

Species Available: Feral hog, squirrels and rabbit.
Acreage: 40,920

Richland Creek WMA

1670 FM 488
Streetman, TX 75859
903-389-7080

Species Available: Whitetail deer and feral hog.
Acreage: 13,796

Sam Houston National Forest WMA

P.O. Box 868
Livingston, TX 77351
936-327-8487

Species Available: Whitetail deer, feral hog and squirrel.
Acreage: 162,854

Sierra Diablo WMA

109 S. Cockrell
Alpine, TX 79830
432-837-3251

Species Available: Big horn sheep
Acreage: 11,624

Somerville WMA

6280 FM 180
Ledbetter, TX 78946
979-289-2392

Species Available: Whitetail deer, feral hog and squirrel.
Acreage: 3,180

Tawakoni WMA

21187 CR 4106
Lindale, TX 75771
903-881-8233

Species Available: Whitetail deer and feral hog.
Acreage: 2,335

Tony Houseman WMA

10 Parks & Wildlife Dr.
Port Arthur, TX 77640
409-736-2551

Species Available: Whitetail deer, feral hog, squirrel and predators.
Acreage: 3,313

Walter Buck WMA

1205 College St.
Junction, TX 76849
325-446-3617

Species Available: Whitetail deer, feral hog and exotics.
Acreage: 2,123

White Oak Creek WMA

33948 HWY 77
Omaha, TX 75571
903-884-3800

Species Available: Whitetail deer, feral hog, rabbit, squirrel and furbearers.
Acreage: 25,777

This Land is Your Land

Texas Parks and Wildlife personnel in charge of public hunting go out of their way to assist hunters in being successful. In addition to offering advice on the best places to hunt within the area they manage, most personnel will assist hunters in game retrieval, skinning, taking trophy pictures or recommending nearby places to stay or eat. None of this extra help and courtesy is contractual. Most personnel offer extra assistance because they love their job and want to see hunters go home happy and with a positive feeling about how their state land is operated. Hunters should do everything they can to return the favor.

While it is true that citizens basically *own* the public land they are using, they do not *own* the employees that work there. A little common courtesy and understanding on the hunter's part will go a long way in how they and the other members of their party are treated.

State operated land in Texas is understaffed and underfunded and no one understands that better than the people who work there on a full-time basis. Showing personnel the same courtesy and understanding that you would like shown to you if the positions were reversed is not only the polite thing to do but may get you a few extra pointers on where and how to take that trophy of a lifetime.

OTHER PUBLIC HUNTING OPPORTUNITIES

In addition to the land managed by Texas Parks and Wildlife, hunting opportunities are also made available on land owned and operated by the Federal Government, the Army Corps of Engineers, various river authorities and several city municipalities. Access to the land varies from lottery type drawing to on-site registration.

Hunters interested in hunting any of the following areas should contact the governing body for more information.

Amistad National Recreation Area

National Park Service
HCR 3, Box 5J
Highway 90 West
Del Rio, TX 78840
830-775-6722
www.nps.gov/amis

Species Available: Whitetail deer, javelina, free range aoudad and mouflon sheep and rabbits.
Acreage: 3,000
Permit Required: $20 annual permit obtained in person only. Hunter Data Sheet must be returned to park personnel or hunters could face $100 violation notice.

Angelina National Forest

111 Walnut Ridge Road
Zavalla, TX 75980
936-897-1068
www.fs.fed.us

Species Available: Whitetail deer, feral hogs, squirrels and rabbits.
Acreage: 153,179

Permit Required: Only a valid Texas hunting license is required to hunt on the property held by Angelina National Forest. However, several Texas WMA lie within or around the forest. TPWD has jurisdiction over these WMAs and different regulations apply therein.

Aransas National Wildlife Refuge

P.O. Box 100
Austwell, TX 77950
361-286-3559
www.fws.gov

Species Available: Whitetail deer and feral hogs.
Acreage: 115,000
Permit Required: Permits issued on a first come, first-served basis.

Balcones Canyonlands National Wildlife Refuge

10711 Burnet Road, Ste. 201
Austin, TX 78758
512-339-9432
www.fws.gov

Species Available: Whitetail deer and feral hogs.
Acreage: 41,000
Permit Required: Permits by application.

Bardwell Lake

4000 Observation Drive
Army Corps of Engineers, Bardwell Project Office
Ennis, TX 75119
972-875-5711
www1.swf-wc.usace.army.mil

Species Available: Feral hogs, squirrels and rabbits.
Acreage: 2,528
Permit Required: Permits obtained at Bardwell Lake office.

Benbrook Lake

P.O. Box 26619
Fort Worth, TX 76126-0619
817-292-2400
www.swf-wc.usace.army.mil

Species Available: Whitetail deer, squirrels and rabbits.
Acreage: 1,400
Permit Required: Permits obtained at Benbrook Lake office.

Big Thicket National Preserve

3785 Milam
Beaumont, TX 77701
409-839-2689
www.nps.gov

Species Available: Whitetail deer, feral hogs, squirrels and rabbits.
Acreage: 97,000
Permit Required: Permits obtained on a first-come, first-served basis.

Canyon Lake

601 COE Road
Canyon Lake, TX 78133
830-964-3341
www.swf-wc.usace.army.mil

Species Available: Whitetail deer
Acreage: 620
Permit Required: Permits by drawing.

Coleto Creek Reservoir

P.O. Box 68
Fannin, TX 77960
361-575-6366
http://www.gbra.org

Species Available: Whitetail deer and feral hogs.
Acreage: 500
Permit Required: Permits by drawing.

Davy Crockett National Forest

Route 1, Box 55 FS
Kennard, TX 75847
936-655-2299
www.fs.fed.us.

Species Available: Whitetail deer, squirrel and rabbits.
Acreage: 162,012
Permit Required: Permits by drawing.

Georgetown Lake

500 Cedar Brakes Road
Georgetown, TX 78628
512-930-5253
http://swf67.swf-wc.usace.army.mil

Species Available: Whitetail deer, squirrel and rabbits.
Acreage: 1,200
Permit Required: Permits by drawing.

Grapevine Lake

110 Fairway Drive
Grapevine, TX 76051
817-481-4544
www1.swf-wc.usace.army.mil

Species Available: Whitetail deer, feral hogs, squirrel and rabbits.
Acreage: 900
Permit Required: Permits by drawing.

Hagerman National Wildlife Refuge

6465 Refuge Road
Sherman, TX 75092
903-786-2826
www.fws.gov

Species Available: Whitetail deer, feral hogs, squirrel and rabbits.
Acreage: 3,000
Permit Required: Permits by drawing.

Laguna Atascosa National Wildlife Refuge

P.O. Box 450
Rio Hondo, TX 78583
956-748-3607
www.fws.gov

Species Available: Free range nilgai, whitetail deer and
feral hogs.
Acreage: 45,000
Permit Required: Permits by drawing.

Lake Meredith National Recreation Area

P.O. Box 1460
Fritch, TX 1460
806-857-3151
www.nps.gov

Species Available: Mule deer, whitetail deer, rabbits, coyotes and raccoon.
Acreage: 50,000
Permit Required: Valid Texas hunting license.

Lake O' the Pines

2669 FM 726
Jefferson, TX 75657
903-665-2336

Species Available: Whitetail deer, feral hog, rabbits and squirrels.
Acreage: 4,500
Permit Required: Valid Texas hunting license.

Lavon Lake

3375 Skyview Drive
Wylie, TX 75098
972-442-3141
www.swf-wc.usace.army.mil

Species Available: Feral hog, rabbits and squirrels.
Acreage: 6,500
Permit Required: Valid Texas hunting license.

L.B.J. National Grasslands
1400 N. Hwy. U.S. 81/U.S. 287
P.O. Box 507
Decatur, TX 76234
www.fs.fed.us

Species Available: Whitetail deer, feral hog, rabbits and squirrels.
Acreage: 20,000
Permit Required: Valid Texas hunting license.

Lewisville Lake
1801 N. Mill St.
Lewisville, TX 75057
972-434-1466
www1.swf-wc.usace.army.mil

Species Available: Feral hog, rabbits and squirrels.
Acreage: 8,000
Permit Required: Permit from Army Corps of Engineer office.

Lower Rio Grande Valley National Wildlife Refuge
Route 2, Box 202A
Alamo, TX 78516
956-784-7500
www.fws.gov

Species Available: Free range nilgai, whitetail deer and feral hog.
Acreage: 4,000
Permit Required: Lower Rio Grande Valley National Wildlife Refuge Special Use Permit.

Navarro Mills Lake

1175 FM 667

Purdon, TX 76679

254-578-1431

www.swf-wc.usace.army.mil

Species Available: Feral hog, squirrels and rabbits.
Acreage: 3,500
Permit Required: Valid Texas Hunting License

O.C. Fisher Lake/ASU Area

3900-2 Mercedes Ave.

San Angelo, TX 76901

915-947-2687

Species Available: Whitetail deer
Acreage: 4,645
Permit Required: By drawing.

Proctor Lake

2180 FM 2861

Comanche, TX 76442

254-879-2424

www.swf-wc.usace.army.mil

Species Available: Squirrels, rabbits
Acreage: 2,500
Permit Required: Permit from Army Corps of Engineer office.

Sabine National Forest

P.O. Box 227
Hemphill, TX 75948
409-787-3870
www.fs.fed.us

Species Available: Whitetail deer, feral hog, squirrels and rabbits.
Acreage: 160,650
Permit Required: Only a valid Texas hunting license is required
to hunt on the property held by Sabine National Forest. However,
several Texas WMAs lie within or around the forest. TPWD has
jurisdiction over these WMAs and different regulations apply
therein.

Sam Rayburn Reservoir

Route 3, Box 486
Jasper, TX 75951
979-596-1622
http://swf67.swf-wc.usace.army.mil

Species Available: Whitetail deer, feral hog, squirrels and rabbits.
Acreage: 6,000
Permit Required: Valid Texas hunting license.

Texoma Lake U.S. Army Corps of Engineers

351 Corps Road
Denison, TX 75020
903-465-4990
www.laketexoma.com

Species Available: Whitetail deer, squirrels and rabbits.
Acreage: 80,000 (Texas and Oklahoma combined)
Permit Required: Valid Texas hunting license.

Town Bluff and B.A. Steinhagen Lake/CEO Area

890 FM 92

Woodville, TX 75979

409-429-3491

www.swf-wc.usace.army.mil

Species Available: Whitetail deer, feral hog, squirrels and rabbits.

Acreage: 875

Permit Required: Valid Texas hunting license.

Truscott Brine Lake

13176 CR 2631

Crowell, TX 79260

940-474-3293

www.swt.usace.army.mil

Species Available: Feral hog

Acreage: 2,000

Permit Required: Valid Texas hunting license.

Waco Lake

3801 Zoo Park Road

Waco, TX 76708

254-756-5359

www.swf-wc.usace.army.mil

Species Available: Whitetail deer, feral hog, squirrels and rabbits.

Acreage: 2,000

Permit Required: Drawing by permit.

Whitney Lake/COE Area

285 CR 3602

Clifton, TX 76634

254-694-3189

www.swf-wc.usace.army.mil

Species Available: Whitetail deer, feral hog, squirrels and rabbits.

Acreage: 14,000

Permit Required: Army Corps permit.

GAME AND HUNTING RANCHES

Game and hunting ranches are becoming more and more popular with hunters because of the advantages they offer over hunting public lands. Perhaps the most distinct advantage that game and hunting ranches offer over WMAs and other public land is that they are man-

The Texas hunting lodge is a place to unwind, make new friends, and talk about hunts past. From left to right, hunter Carlos Celaya, outfitter Garry Wright of Garry Wright Safaris and lodge owner Cynthia Ott all enjoy a bottle of Texas wine.

aged with one objective in mind: to produce quality game. This is accomplished through sound management, supplemental feeding and hard work on the part of the owner and usually with the assistance of a biologist.

Game and hunting ranches, unlike WMAs, are in the business of hunting and the owners of these operations will go out of their way to ensure that their clients have a good time and at least the opportunity of taking a trophy.

The following is a list of some of the larger and more reputable ranches. Contact an individual ranch or guide for species available, current prices and terms of hunt.

Fair Chase, Canned Hunts and Game Ranches

Many people who have not hunted on game or hunting ranches enclosed by a high fence automatically believe the practice to be unsporting and unethical. Even worse, some confuse all hunting taking place on such properties to be "canned." While it is true that some landowners will do anything to make money, the overwhelming majority of hunts that take place behind a high fence are challenging, sporting and above all, fair chase.

The following is a list of criteria that qualifies a high-fenced area as "fair chase," according to Safari Club International. Most reputable game and hunting ranches in Texas follow or exceed the criteria.

- The animals hunted must have freely resided on the property on which they are being hunted for at least six months or longer.
- The hunting property shall provide escape cover that allows the animals to elude hunters for extended periods of time and multiple occurrences. Escape cover, in the form of rugged terrain or topography, and/or dense thickets or

stands of woods, shall collectively comprise at least 50 percent of the property.

- The animals hunted must be part of a breeding herd that is a resident on the hunted property.
- The operators of the preserve must provide freely available and ample amounts of cover, food and water at all times.
- Animals that are to be hunted must exhibit their natural flight/survival instincts.
- No zoo animals, exhibited animals or tame animals are to be hunted.
- No hunting or selling of hunting rights to a specified animal.
- Hunting methods employed cannot include driving, herding or chasing animals to awaiting hunters.
- Every effort must be made to utilize all meat commonly consumed from a taken animal.

777 Ranch

P.O. Box 610
Hondo, TX 78861-0610
830-426-4821
www.777ranch.com

7 Canyons Ranch

P.O. Box 101
Tarpley, TX 78883
830.562.3333
www.7canyonsranch.com

Hunting well managed land can produce excellent trophies such as this trophy axis deer taken by David Diekmann with outfitter Garry Wright near Camp Verde.

Abby Abernathy

C/o Spur Hotel
P.O. Box 1207
Archer City, TX 76351
940-574-2501

Boss Ranch

P.O. Box 72
Marathon, TX 79842
432-395-2490
www.bossranch.com

Buffalo Creek Ranch

P.O. Box 308
Leaky, TX 78873
830-862-1887
www.buffalocreekranch.com

Clear Springs Ranch

8930 State Hwy. 173 South
Bandera, TX 78003
830-796-9100
www.clearspringsranch.com

Double C Ranch / Hunt with Jeff

P.O. Box 86
Crystal City, TX 78839
830-374-2744
www.huntingwithjeff.com

Give Your Guide a Break

When hunting on a game or hunting ranch remember to give your guide enough time alone to tend to his duties. In addition to being the center of your care and entertainment, hunting guides work extremely hard and long hours in order to assure their clients of a fun time and a quality hunt.

In order to make your guide's load slightly easier, and to assure you of the best hunt possible, be sure to give him a break by offering to:

• Have all your required licenses and paper work ready upon your arrival.

- Have a clear and reasonable idea of exactly what kind of hunt you'd like to have (i.e. Are you only interested in a certain size animal? What is your preferred shot distance?).
- Help him in preparing for the day's hunt by loading and unloading the hunting vehicle of game, ice chests, food, trash and other goods.
- Open and close ranch gates.

Remember, just because you are offering to help doesn't mean your guide will necessarily take you up on the offer. Truth be told, he might be able to do his job better and faster without your help. Regardless, offering to provide help never hurt anyone's feelings.

Sometimes the best way to assist your guide is by not doing things. Such as:

- Don't expect him to entertain you constantly, especially in the evening. Asking him to have one or two drinks with you in the evening is fine; asking him to entertain you all night is not (he has to get up long before you do).
- Don't ask him to do anything immoral, illegal or that he has already stated he won't do.
- Don't tell him the best way to hunt an area (he hunts the area for a living; he knows what he's doing).
- Don't forget to give him a tip of between 10 and 20 percent, if not more.

Garry Wright Safaris

P.O. Box 901
Fredericksburg, TX 78624
830-9901362
www.garrywright.com

Greystone Castle

P.O. Box 158
Mingus, TX 76463
254-672-5927
www.greystonecastle.com

Joshua Creek Ranch

P.O. Box 1946
Boerne, TX 78006
830-537-5090
www.joshuacreek.com

Indianhead Ranch

HCR 1, Box 102
Del Rio, TX 78840
830-775-6481
www.indianheadranch.com

Las Auras Ranch

220 Hillside Road
Laredo, TX 78041
956-722-1012
www.texas-hunts.com

The metal buzzards awaiting hunters at Las Auras Ranch
make for one of the more interesting ranch entrances in Texas.

Rock Creek Ranch

2726 Miller

Port Neches, TX 77651

409.727.4556

http://huntrockcreekranch.com

South Texas Outfitters/Hog Hunting Texas

P.O. Box 1121

Pearsall, TX 78061

830-466-5294 or 5295

Y.O. Ranch

1736 Y.O. Ranch Road

Mountain Home, TX 78058

830-640-2624

www.yoranch.net

8

HUNTING, CONSERVATION &
SCORING ORGANIZATIONS

The following groups help promote and secure hunting and hunting rights through a variety of methods such as conservation and hunting projects, public relations, legal defense and lobbying. Contact individual organizations to obtain more information.

Boone & Crockett

250 Station Drive
Missoula, MT 59801
406-542-1888
www.boone-crockett.org

Dallas Safari Club

6390 LBJ Freeway, Suite 108
Dallas, TX 75240
972-980-9800
www.biggame.org

Foundation for North American Wild Sheep

720 Allen Ave
Cody, WY 82414-3402
307-527-6261
www.fnaws.org

Houston Safari Club

4615 Southwest Freeway, Suite 805
Houston, TX 77027
713-623-8844
www.houstonsafariclub.org

Lone Star Bowhunters Association

117 Hwy 332 W. Suite J, #101
Lake Jackson, TX 77566
361-571-5627
www.lonestarbowhunter.com

Los Cazadores

490 South IH 35
Pearsall, TX 76240
830-334-5959
www.loscazadores.com

Mule Deer Foundation

1005 Terminal Way, Suite 170
Reno, NV 89502
775-322-6558
888-375-DEER
www.muledeer.org

Pope and Young Club

273 Mill Creek Road

P.O. Box 548

Chatfield, MN 55923

507-867-4144

www.pope-young.org

Records of Exotics

P.O. Box 502

Ingram, TX 78025

830-367-5568

www.roe.texaswildlife.net

Rowland Ward

P.O. Box 1222

Spotsylvania, VA 22553

540-710-7234

www.rowlandward.com

Safari Club International

4800 West Gates Pass Road

Tucson, AZ 85745-9490

520-620-1220

www.safariclub.org

Texas Bighorn Society

c/o Charles Wolcott

3832 Hanover Avenue

Dallas, TX 75225-7116

214-891-0987

www.texasbighornsociety.org

Texas Exotic Wildlife Association

105 Henderson Branch Road W.

Ingram, TX 78025

830-367-7761

www.exoticwildlifeassociation.com

Texas State Rifle Association

4570 Westgrove Drive, Suite 200

Addison, TX 75001-3222

972-889-8772

www.tsra.com

Texas Trophy Hunters Association

P.O. Box 791107

San Antonio, TX 78279-1107

210-523-8500

www.ttha.com

Texas Wildlife Association

2800 NE Loop 410, Suite 105

San Antonio, TX 78218

210-826-2904

www.texas-wildlife.org

Trophy Game Records of the World

1600 Harper Rd Ste 104

Kerrville, TX 78028-9114

830-895-4997

www.exoticwildlifeassociation.com

Weiser Weight and Tusk

4188 CR 211

Halletsville, TX 77964

361-772-8023

www.brutalboarcreations.com

SCORING ORGANIZATIONS

Several conservation and pro-hunting organizations such as Boone & Crockett, Safari Club International, Rowland Ward and a host of others have established scoring systems that encourage members to rank their animals. For some hunters this is a way to take the sport to a competitive level by allowing them to judge and compare their trophy against those of other members. For others it is a way to get their name in a record book and support their organization. And still other hunters just think that scoring their trophy is fun.

While the scoring methods vary from organization to organization, most consist of a cumulative score based on the measurements of the animal's most desired attributes—tusks, antlers or horns. Some, such as Weiser Weight and Tusk which deals exclusively with wild boar, combine the animal's measurements with its weight to gage a score.

Hunters who are interested in scoring their animal should contact the organization they are interested in for the latest information on scoring regulations and minimum entry qualifications.

9

Manufacturers Listing

The following manufacturers produce what I believe to be the best hunting equipment. Products from these companies have made my hunting and writing career much easier, safer and comfortable.

Beretta Gallery Dallas

One of only two galleries in the United States, this store carries the best of Beretta's legendary firearms, clothing, gifts and accessories.
41 Highland Park Village
Dallas, TX 75205
214-559-9800
www.beretta.com

Blackhawk

Military grade hunting packs, belts, slings, knives, flashlights and accessories.
4850 Brookside Court
Norfolk, VA 23502
800-694-5263
www.blackhawk.com

Boyt Harness Company

Makers of exceptional gun cases, hunting accessories and safari clothing.
Boyt Harness Company
One Boyt Drive
Osceola, IA 50213
800-550-2698
www.boytharness.com

Briley

Shooting accessories and tools, clothing and custom gun work.
1230 Lumpkin Rd.
Houston, TX 77043
800-331-5718
www.briley.com

Browning

*Makers of excellent firearms, safes, gun cases, clothing, lights
and knives for more than 100 years.*
One Browning Place
Morgan, UT 84050
800-333-3288
www.browning.com

Brush Country Camo

Makers of exceptional camouflage clothing and outdoor accessories.
P.O. Box 4314
Bryan, TX 77805
877-599-7225
www.brushcountrycamo.com

Bushlan

Another manufacturer of exceptional camouflage clothing and outdoor accessories.
The Disappearing Act
5912 San Bernardo Suite 500
Laredo, TX 78041
866-296-2266
www.bushlan.com

Cannon/Safari Safes

Solid, dependable, tough safes for firearms and memories of the hunt.
216 South 2nd Avenue
Building 932
San Bernardino, CA 92408
800-222-1055
www.canonsafe.com
www.safarisafe.com

CZ USA

Exceptionally rugged, durable and dependable firearms.
P.O. Box 171073
Kansas City, KS 66117-0073
800-955-4486
www.cz-usa.com

ELCAN Optical Technologies

Maker of the first digital riflescope.
1601 N. Plano Road
Richardson, TX 75081
1-877-893-5226
www.elcansportingoptics.com

Gander MTN.

Retailer that offers just about anything and everything a hunter could ever need.

Stores in Amarillo, Beaumont, Corsicana, Houston, Spring, Sherman, Sugarland, Texarkana and Tyler.

www.gandermountain.com

Garmin International Inc.

Cutting edge GPS units.

1200 East 151st Street

Olathe, KS 66062-3426

913-397-8200

www.garmin.com

GunSafe

Beautifully crafted wooden gun safes with hidden metal rods to keep firearms safe and secure.

160 E. CR 240 N.

Arthur, IL 61911

877-4gunsafe

http://classicpressroom.com

Leaf River Outdoor Products

Makers of some of the best game cameras on the market today.

VibraShine Inc.

P.O. Box 557

Taylorsville, MS 39168

601-785-9854

www.vibrashine.com

Liberty Safe

Heavy duty safes for sportsmen and collectors.
Liberty Safe of Texas, Inc.
614 Easy Street
Garland, TX 75042
972-272-9788
www.agunsafe.com

Leica

Superb optics, riflescopes and rangefinders.
1 Pearl Ct., Unit A
Allendale, NJ 07401
201-995-0051
www.leicacamerausa.com

Long Grass Outfitters

Safari style clothing, shooting accessories, jewelry and books.
Long Grass Outfitters
12019 Bammel
San Antonio, TX 78231
210-408-6402
www.long-grass.com

Meopta Sports Optics USA

By far the best sporting optics I have ever used.
50 Davids Drive
Hauppauge, NY 11788
866-789-0555
www.meopta.com

Miz Mac Designs

Hunting and shooting apparel designed for women.
Miz Mac Designs
P.O. Box 81
Roundhead, OH 43336
877-568-2529
www.mizmac.com

Murray Leather

Craftsmen of quality, functional and beautiful leather slings, cartridge belts, scabbards and bags.
P.O. Box 373
Aledo, TX 76008
817-441-7480
www.murrayleather.com

Nikon

For more than 90 years, the makers of the finest binoculars, spotting scopesriflescopes, handgun and shotgun scopes and rangefinders.
1300 Walt Whitman Rd.
Melville, NY 11747-3064
800-247-3464
www.nikonsportoptics.com

Red Oxx

Makers of the best travel and adventure bags on the market today. My favorite.
310 North 13th St.
Billings, MT, 59101
1-888-RED-OXXX
www.redoxx.com

Remington

Legendary firearm and ammunition manufacturer. My only ammunition.

P.O. Box 700

Madison, NC 27025-0700

336-548-8577

www.remington.com

Russell Moccasin Co.

Custom boots that will handle even the toughest terrain Texas can dish out.

285 S.W. Franklin

P.O. Box 309

Berlin, WI 54923-0309

920-361-2252

www.russellmoccasin.com

She Safari

Hunting apparel designed specifically for women.

10313 Autumn Run Ln.

Conroe, TX 77304

936-756-7169

www.shesafari.com

SOG

Quality knives and cutlery.

6521 212th St. SW

Lynnwood, WA 98036

425-771-6230

www.sogknives.com

Streamlight

Exceptional flashlights.
Streamlight Inc.
30 Eagleville Road
Eagelville, PA 19403
800-523-7488
www.streamlight.com

Surefire

The innovator in LED flashlights.
18300 Mt. Baldy Circle
Fountain Valley, CA 92708-6122
714-545-9444
www.surefire.com

TAG Safari

Safari wear that is as at home in Texas as it is in Africa.
Comfortable and resilient.
Africa Safaris & Outdoor Importers Inc.
West 10 Business Center
1008 Wirt Rd., Suite 120
Houston, TX 77055
713-688-3424
www.tagsafari.com

Texas Hunt Company

Superb hunting accessories, scabbards, gun cases and packs all designed to withstand the unforgiving Texas environment.

Texas Hunt Co.

P.O. Box 10

Monahans, TX 79756

888-894-8682

www.texashuntco.com

Texas Safari Hunting Products

Quality safari wear with a Texas twist.

6710 Walton Heath

Houston, TX 77069

713-202-9329

www.texassafarihuntingproducts.com

T.Z. Case International

Safe and secure firearm cases.

1786 Curtiss Court

La Verne, CA 91750

909-392-8806

www.tz-case.com

Walden & Bork

Masters of leather tooling and turning game skins into works of art.

N7453 Cty. Rd. QQ

Prescott, WI 54021

1-715-425-7779

www.waldenbork.com

Walker's Game Ear

The original and best hearing protection on the market.
P.O. Box 1069
Media, PA 19063
610-565-8952
www.walkersgameear.com

Westley Richards

For more than 200 years, makers of legendary firearms, ammunition, accessories, leather goods, luggage and clothing.
Westley Richards USA
3810 Valley Commons Drive
Suite 2
Bozeman, MT 59718
406-586-1946
www.westleyrichards.com

What-A-Jeep

Experts at converting Jeeps into Texas Safari style hunting vehicles.
4901 Hillside
Building C
Amarillo, TX 79109
806-322-0354

PHOTOGRAPHY & ILLUSTRATION CREDITS

Front Matter
Page v, Gayne C. Young

Chapter 1
All Texas maps are based on Gould, F.W., G.O. Hoffman, and C. A. Rechenthin
Page 2, Texas Parks and Wildlife Department
Page 4, Texas Parks and Wildlife Department
Page 5, Texas Parks and Wildlife Department
Page 8, Texas Parks and Wildlife Department
Page 10, Texas Parks and Wildlife Department
Page 11, Texas Parks and Wildlife Department
Page 15, Texas Parks and Wildlife Department
Page 18, Texas Parks and Wildlife Department
Page 20, Texas Parks and Wildlife Department
Page 21, Texas Parks and Wildlife Department

Chapter 2
Page 24, Texas Parks and Wildlife Department
Page 26, Texas Parks and Wildlife Department
Page 27, Younger Brothers Blinds
Page 29, Texas Parks and Wildlife Department
Page 30, Gayne C. Young
Page 33, Texas Parks and Wildlife Department
Page 35, Texas Parks and Wildlife Department
Page 36, Texas Parks and Wildlife Department
Page 37, Texas Parks and Wildlife Department
Page 38, What-a-Jeep
Page 40, Gayne C. Young
Page 42, Jessie Martinez, Bushlan Camo
Page 43, Texas Parks and Wildlife Department
Page 45, Gayne C. Young

Chapter 3

Page 106, Texas Parks and Wildlife Department

Chapter 4

Page 110, U.S. Fish and Wildlife Service

Page 113, Texas Parks and Wildlife Department

Page 120, U.S. Fish and Wildlife Service

Page 122, Gayne C. Young

Page 124, Gayne C. Young

Page 125, Texas Parks and Wildlife Department

Page 127, Texas Parks and Wildlife Department

Page 128, Texas Parks and Wildlife Department

Page 129, Texas Parks and Wildlife Department

Page 131, U.S. Fish and Wildlife Service

Page 133, Terry Spivey, USDA Forest Service

Page 136, Texas Parks and Wildlife Department

Page 140, Texas Parks and Wildlife Department

Page 143, Texas Parks and Wildlife Department

Chapter 5

Page 157, Daniel Wojcik

Page 158, Texas Department of Transportation

Page 159, Hansell F. Cross, Georgia State University

Page 160, Jim Occi

Page 161, Lacy L. Hyche, Auburn University

Page 162, Texas Parks and Wildlife Department

Page 164, Whitney Cranshaw, Colorado State University

Page 165 (top), Jerry A. Payne, USDA Agricultural Research Service

Page 165, (bottom)Scott Bauer, USDA Agricultural Research Service

Page 167, Texas Parks and Wildlife Department

Page 169, Texas Parks and Wildlife Department

Page 171, Texas Parks and Wildlife Department

Page 173, Texas Parks and Wildlife Department

Page 174, Jeffrey J. Jackson, University of Georgia

RECOMMENDED BOOKS & WORKS CITED

Alvarez, Elizabeth Cruce, ed. *Texas Almanac: 2004-2005.* College Station, Texas: Texas A&M University Press Consortium, 2004.

Ayala, Chris. Personal interview. 11 January 2007.

Bartlett, Richard, Joanne Krieger and Jack Unruh. *The Sportsman's Guide to Texas.* Dallas: Taylor Publishing Company, 1988.

Behler, John L. and F. Wayne King, ed. *National Audubon Society Field Guide to North American Reptiles & Amphibians.* Syracuse, New York: Chanticleer Press, Inc., 1995.

Bomar, George W. *Texas Weather.* Austin, Texas: University of Texas Press, 1995.

Boone, Kathy. "Proof's in the Pudding." *Texas Bighorn Society: Bighorn* (Winter 2004).

Brock-Clutton, Juliet and Don E. Wilson, ed. *Mammals.* New York: D.K. Publishing, Inc., 2002.

"Commonly Asked Questions About BSE in Products Regulated by FDA's Center for Food Safety and Applied Nutrition (CFSAN)." *U.S. Food and Drug Administration* (11 July 2006).

Davis, William B. and David J. Schmidly. *The Mammals of Texas.* Austin, Texas: Texas Parks and Wildlife Press, 1994.

"DSHS Issues Plague Precautions for Midland County Area." *Texas Department of State Health Services* (10 July 2006).

Drees, Bastiaan M. and John A. Jackman. *A Field Guide to Common Texas Insects.* Houston, Texas: Gulf Publishing Company, 1998.

Faw, Michael D. "Worth the Cost." *Sports Afield* (June/July 2006): 39.

"Herps of Texas." *Texas Memorial Museum* (10 January 2005).

Halse, A.R.D., ed. *Rowland Ward's Sportsman's Handbook: XV Edition.* Houghton, South Africa: Rowland Ward Publications, 2003.

House, Boyce. *I Give You Texas!* San Antonio, Texas: The Naylor Company, 1943.

Jackman, John A. "Spiders." *Texas Agricultural Extension Service* (1 January 2006).

Jumper, Eric. Telephone interview. 30 May 2006.

Letcher, Owen. *Big Game Hunting in North-Eastern Rhodesia.* New York: St. Martin's Press, 1987.

Leggett, Mike. "A Breed Apart." *Austin American-Statesman* (7 November 2004): A1+.

"List of Wildlife Management Areas in Texas, Ordered by County." *Texas Parks and Wildlife* (26 August 2004).

"Local Transmission of Plasmodium vivax Malaria—Houston, Texas, 1994." *Center for Disease Control and Prevention* (22 January 2006).

Luger, Doug. Telephone interview. 5 June 2006.

Martin, Jeff. Personal interview. 18 January 2005.

"Mexican Gray Wolf." *Fossil Rim Wildlife Center* (25 January 2005).

Mills, Buddy. Personal interview. 16 March 2005.

"Mountain Lion (Puma concolor)." *The Cyber Zoomobile* (16 January 2005).

Pelton, Robert Young, et al. *The World's Most Dangerous Places.* Redondo Beach, California: Fielding Worldwide, Inc., 1997.

"Return of the Black Bear." *Big Bend National Park* (23 January 2005).

Safari Club International. *SCI Record Book of Trophy Animals: Edition XI, Vol. 1, African Field Edition.*

Safari Club International. *SCI Record Book of Trophy Animals: Edition XI, Vol. 2, African Field Edition.*

Safari Club International. *SCI Record Book of Trophy Animals: Edition XI, Vol. 3, South America, Europe, Asia, South Pacific.*

Schmidly, David J. *Texas Natural History: A Century of Change.* Lubbock, Texas: Texas Tech University Press, 2002.

Temple, Thompson. *Field Guide to North American Exotic Game.* Ingram, Texas: Record of Exotics, 2005.

"The Rut in White-tailed Deer." *Texas Parks and Wildlife* (22 January 2006).

The Ultimate Ungulate Page. Brent Huffman. 22 January 2005. www.ultimateungulate.com.

Vine, Katy. "Monster Inc." *Texas Monthly* (October 2005): 64-74.

Weishuhn, Larry. "Understanding the Rut." *Game & Fish* (2 February 2006).

Weniger, Del. *The Explorers' Texas: Volume 2 The Animals They Found.* Austin, Texas: Eakin Press, 1996.

"West Nile Virus." *Texas Department of Health* (2 May 2006).

"Wildlife Making Texas Highways Hazardous." *Insurance Journal* (9 January 2006).

Wilson, Ken. Personal interview. 30 May 2006.

Wright, Garry. Personal interview. 5 June 2006.

8